IS SPANISH
·FOR·
"PELICAN"

ALCATRAZ, CALIF.

To
Tricia

P. T. Mahony

1956 To 1963

Assignment
ALCATRAZ

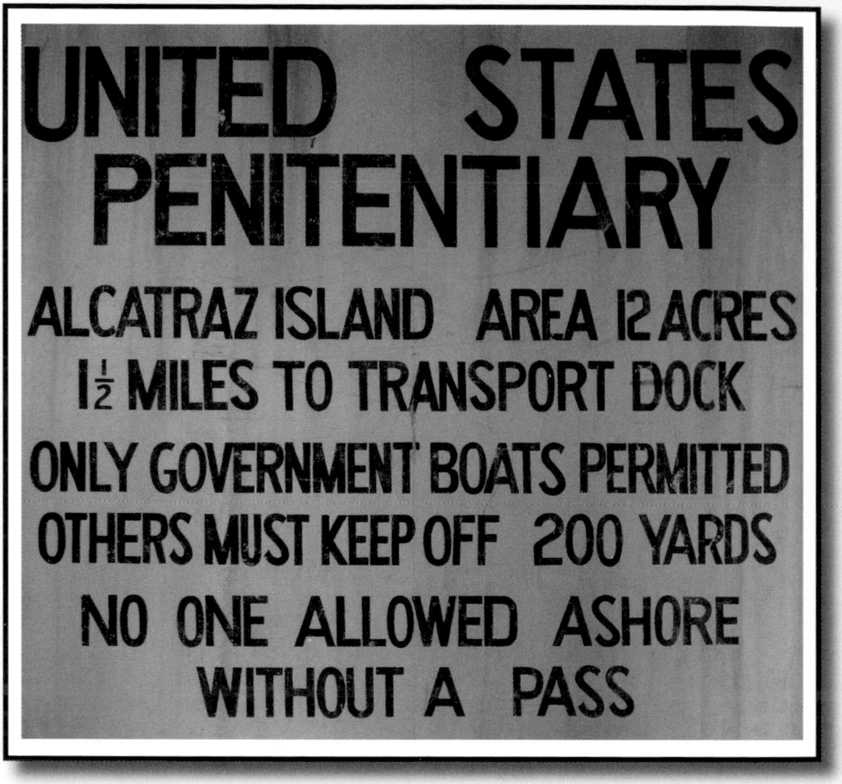
UNITED STATES
PENITENTIARY
ALCATRAZ ISLAND AREA 12 ACRES
1½ MILES TO TRANSPORT DOCK
ONLY GOVERNMENT BOATS PERMITTED
OTHERS MUST KEEP OFF 200 YARDS
NO ONE ALLOWED ASHORE
WITHOUT A PASS

ASSIGNMENT ALCATRAZ

My Dirty, Wonderful Job

PATRICK MAHONEY

CORRECTIONAL OFFICER
& PRISON LAUNCH CAPTAIN

GOLDEN GATE NATIONAL PARKS CONSERVANCY
SAN FRANCISCO, CALIFORNIA

Golden Gate National Parks Conservancy
Building 201 Fort Mason, San Francisco, California 94123
www.parksconservancy.org

ISBN 978-1-932519-25-9

Library of Congress Control Number: 2012954095

Design: Vivian Young
Editor: Susan Tasaki
Production Manager: Sarah Lau Levitt
Historical Review: Michael Esslinger
Development: Robert Lieber

Photos used in this book come from a variety of sources, some of which may require permission to reproduce.

Unless noted below, all photographs are from Golden Gate National Recreation Area/ Park Archives and Records Center.

Alcatraz Alumni Association Collection: p. 133 (top)
Collier's Magazine (August 6, 1954): pp. 100 (bottom), 117
Phil Dollison Collection: pp. 55 (bottom), 58 (bottom), 99 (top), 100 (top), 109
Golden Gate National Parks Conservancy: p. 56 (diagrams)
Bill Long Collection: pp. 6, 55 (top), 57 (bottom), 60–61, 79 (top), 80–83, 85, 86, 99 (bottom), 101, 104, 133 (bottom), 134–135
Pat Mahoney Collection: pp. 63, 64, 78, 118

Printed in Hong Kong

PARKS FOR ALL FOREVER™

The Golden Gate National Parks Conservancy is the nonprofit membership organization created to preserve the Golden Gate National Parks, enhance the experiences of park visitors, and build a community dedicated to conserving the parks for the future. Find out more at *www.parksconservancy.org* and at *www.nps.gov.*

CONTENTS

ACKNOWLEDGMENTS

To my wife Anna, who lived and loved our life together on Alcatraz.

To my dear friend Darla Bycott, who supported and encouraged my efforts to write this book.

To my long-time friend, Bill Long, for allowing us to include pictures from his time on Alcatraz and sharing his stories with us.

To Steve and Yanny Mahoney, for writing a chapter for the book on Steve's time as a child on the island (and without whose help this project would never have been completed).

To Cathryn Mahoney for her transcribing, researching, and editing efforts, and for being a wonderful granddaughter—go Air Force!

To Thomas Mahoney for his editing efforts, and for being a great grandson—go Army!

To my friend Tom Reeves, for providing stories about his time as a young man on the Rock.

Thanks to many others as well, including Phil Dollison, Jim Albright, Jerry Champion, and other members of the Alcatraz Alumni Association.

And a special thanks to the National Park Service staff at Alcatraz and members of the Golden Gate National Parks Conservancy for support and encouragement throughout this project.

My thanks to you all.

INTRODUCTION

This story began when I entered the prison service at United States Penitentiary Alcatraz Island back in 1956 and, with my young wife (and later, our children), began life in a unique and exciting place. During my seven years on the island, we developed strong bonds of friendship with the families living there; there was also respect between the guards and the hardened criminals serving time in the toughest prison in the nation.

This book is the story of our friends, life around the inmates, and my time as captain of the USP Alcatraz Island launch. It also includes the bittersweet experience of captaining the boat that carried the last of the inmates away from the island on March 21, 1963. I hope you enjoy these stories, and come to see Alcatraz not just as a former prison, but also as a place families treasured as a special part of their lives.

A job at Alcatraz was an opportunity of a lifetime, and it was actually safer than my previous jobs as a mineworker. As a guard—or correctional officer, as we were formally known—I found at Alcatraz a stable and decent way to earn a living. My wife was thrilled with the opportunity to live in one of the most beautiful settings in the world at one-quarter of the normal rental rate, in a thriving, fun-loving community where we created close friendships.

After coming back from the war in Korea, I also found it to be a great new opportunity, and another chance to serve my country. Of course, I couldn't know what lay ahead, and from the beginning, the daily challenges of working with convicts in a maximum-security prison reminded me how different this job was from any other I'd ever had.

I have a big heart, but I'm also a tough guy. I had to be, otherwise I couldn't do the jobs I did. It's the Irish in me, I guess. You're not going to hear a lot about feelings; I don't go in for that touchy-feely stuff. Not my generation. But you will hear about honor, decency, and doing the right thing by my fellow man. My compassion came out in the way I treated the prisoners. I'm also not going to tell you how much I loved my wife Anna. She was a fine woman, and she raised my wonderful kids. When she departed, she left a hole in my heart that will be there forever.

My family lived in Colorado, and I was one of six brothers. After finishing up military service in Korea, I worked in law enforcement under my father, Thomas Mahoney, sheriff of San Miguel County, Colorado. I had known Anna, the woman who became my wife and companion, since grammar school, and we married on Valentine's Day 1954. Soon after, I took mining jobs in Colorado and Death Valley, California, where the pay was good. Anna was my helpmate throughout, often working as payroll clerk for the companies that employed me as a contract miner. But eventually, we came to see that mining was just too dangerous. In addition to the inherent risks, mines were always situated in communities of gun-toters, fearless and desperate men. Of course, I was later to meet fearless and desperate men on Alcatraz, but there was a big difference: at Alcatraz, they had no weapons and were confined to cells.

Eventually, I landed a job at Mare Island in the northern corner of San Francisco Bay, welding atomic submarines for the US Navy. It was a good place to acquire mechanical skills. Anna and I lived just across the channel in Vallejo. When I heard there were openings at the penitentiary on Alcatraz, I became keenly interested. This opportunity would make use of both my experience working in law enforcement and my mechanical skills.

Less than a month after my initial interview, Warden Paul J. Madigan hired me. I commuted from Vallejo to San Francisco for a while, but once an apartment was available in Building 64 (originally an army barracks built in the 1860s), we moved to the island.

When I applied for a job at USP Alcatraz in 1956, I was told that I would need to undergo physical endurance tests, very much like military boot camp. But it wasn't like that for me after all. While Madigan was interested in my previous experience in law enforcement, my mechanical skills were in such demand that I never had to do push-ups to prove myself as a correctional officer. The endurance tests were waived, too.

My training for guard duty was also atypical. What should have taken ten days to two weeks took eighteen months. And not because I was a slow learner. A new correctional officer was required to spend one day in each of these locations: the control room, clothing room, cellhouse, kitchen, gun galleries, and in each of towers 1, 2, and 3. He also had to spend a day on the dock and learn how to X-ray all the food that came in by boat. Time in the prison industries, which included the laundry, shoe shop, tailor and glove shops, and brush and furniture factories, was also part of every newcomer's initiation.

Since I was constantly being taken away from these standard duties to fill in as a mechanic in some other part of the prison, my "break-in" period was extended. The prison already had a mechanic, Clifford Fish, but he suffered from acrophobia and could not climb the towers or venture up into other high areas. I became his backup, since I wasn't afflicted that way.

Despite what others might think, being a correctional officer on Alcatraz wasn't a grim job; it was secure and had many benefits, and I was happy in my work. Furthermore I was convinced that I was providing a service to the community.

Anna settled into the island community and cared for our three sons—Steve and the twins, Mike and Pat (Mike and Pat were USP Alcatraz's last set of twins)—all of whom came into the world during my seven years there. She also commuted every day to her job at Fireman's Fund Insurance Company in San Francisco.

At the end of my shift, I couldn't wait to go home and tell Anna what had happened. There was always a good story to relate, and she was always eager to hear it. Here are some of those stories.

SECTION ONE

ON THE JOB

On duty in the control center.

On my first day at USP Alcatraz, I was told to go to the isolation unit and escort a prisoner from his cell to the office of the assistant warden, who would review his status. Two other correctional officers were waiting for me in D Block, the isolation cellblock, and they led me to the heavy, double-doored cell of the convict in question. I was to go into the dark cell and bring him out. I vaguely noticed that the other officers stood back as I unlocked the outer door.

When I cracked the door a bit, the foulest stench hit me in the face. Once the entryway door was fully open, I could see that the prisoner had plastered himself, the walls, and the floor with his feces. I staggered back, sure I was going to lose my breakfast, but managed to control myself. As the inmate stood slathered in his waste, a sly smile crept across his face—it was his mocking way of signaling what he thought of us.

In hindsight, it's easy to see that my colleagues knew precisely what they were doing when they summoned me. They had seen this convict's performance before, and I was the newcomer. You might say that I was being initiated—kind of like pledging a fraternity.

I told the man to come forward and head to the showers, and was relieved that he walked out of his cell voluntarily and without protest. Had he rebelled, I would have had to take hold of him in some way. My colleagues pulled two convicts from other cells in isolation and ordered them to scour the stinking compartment. With buckets and a hose, they mopped for several hours. In return, they got a change of clothing.

The rebellious inmate was appearing before the associate warden (AW) that day to review a previous offense. The AW would determine how long the convict was going to spend in isolation before he could return to the general population. However, now he had more mischief to account for. When the AW asked him why he fouled his cell, he explained that he thought his behavior would make him seem insane, and this would qualify him for the US Medical Center for Federal Prisoners in Springfield, Missouri, which included a hospital for the mentally ill. He thought he would get softer treatment there. In fact, what he got was more time where he had been: in the "hole," the dark section of isolation where incorrigible prisoners were kept without light, furniture, or the means to communicate.

That was the outlandish first day of what was to become a fulfilling and exciting career. I didn't let that smelly experience scare me away.

How did this inhospitable piece of real estate come to inflame the imaginations and emotions of people the world over? Before it was a maximum-security federal penitentiary, Alcatraz was a military prison. When the army decided to vacate the island in the early 1930s, it was transferred to the Department of Justice (DOJ), which had been looking for a place that could hold the nation's "worst of the worst" criminals and act as a deterrent to others. Overseen by the newly created Bureau of Prisons (BOP), the massive concrete prison building that the army had constructed in the early twentieth century was refurbished, guard towers were added, and fencing and other barriers were reconfigured. The most modern security apparatus of the day was installed in the cellhouse.

A Walk around the Prison

To visualize the prison's layout, see page 56. The main cellhouse had four parallel rows of three-tiered cell blocks (A, B, C, and D), divided by corridors. In the 1930s refurbishing, A Block had been left much as it was during the army days. D Block, which had been rebuilt in 1940 after a particularly daring escape, was used to isolate prisoners for a variety of reasons. Some men were there for short periods, while others, like the "Birdman of Alcatraz" Robert Stroud, spent almost all of his time on the Rock in a D Block cell.

During the federal-prison years, most of the prisoners were housed in B and C Blocks' 336 cells. The average population was around 280; more than that were tough to manage. The main corridor between B and C Blocks was dubbed "Broadway," and the corridor between C and D Blocks was "Seedy Street."

The mechanism that controlled the cell doors had been installed by Stewart Iron Works of Covington, Kentucky, which had borrowed some of its technology from locking devices used in Pullman trains. The officer in charge of the door-opening mechanism could open an entire row of cell fronts, or just a single cell. At the other end of the cellblock, another officer operated a similar control. Meanwhile, unarmed guards walked the floors and tiers throughout the cellhouse. It was in such an environment that the daily life of the prison took place.

Prison Life

Broadway was pretty quiet unless somebody was on a rampage, which didn't happen very often. However, one of the inmates, Jerry Clymore (AZ-1339), had it in for me, and he changed the acoustics in the cellhouse for a while. I was supervising cleanup duty in the dining room, where Clymore's job was to clean tables. He wasn't working as efficiently or as speedily as I would have liked, so I pressed him to work a little harder. Apparently he didn't care for that.

About this time, I began noticing that as I walked through the cellhouse, the inmates would yell out, "Three cheers for Mahoney! Shit, shit, shit!" This happened several times, but I couldn't tell who was the instigator. Then I walked by Clymore's cell just in time to hear him call out, "Three cheers for Mahoney!" The other inmates responded: "Shit, shit, shit!" and I knew who had started these shenanigans. I stopped and asked him, "This was your idea, wasn't it?" He responded, "It wasn't me, Mr. Mahoney, that wasn't me." "Jerry, you're not going to the yard this weekend," I told him. I had him locked up for the weekend so he could think twice about it.

The Yard

Most prisoners went to the recreation yard daily for a couple of hours after they finished their work. On weekends, there could be as many as two hundred men in that enclosure at the same time. (Those in isolation lost their yard privileges.)

In the yard, convicts could play chess or baseball, walk, or sit on the cement bleachers and look at San Francisco, a mile and a quarter across the bay. Most importantly, they used the time to talk amongst themselves. A frequent topic of conversation was the progress of their legal cases and their activities with their lawyers. Prisoners usually didn't want other people to overhear or interrupt their conversations about their legal-defense preparations.

Some convicts became real experts on federal law. The dignified Courtney Taylor (AZ-1038) was very astute on the subject. He would go into great detail with other convicts about their defense preparation. While he wore the same prison uniform as everyone else, Taylor looked very sharp. He did a lot of law favors for other convicts, so his laundry received special attention, and he was always immaculately turned out.

Keeping Track

In addition to thirteen scheduled inmate counts, we made frequent random counts throughout the day and night. Part of this was, of course, to verify that everyone was where he should be, but it was also another way to stay alert to prisoners' activities in their cells. For example, if I passed a cell and saw that a man had rolled up his mattress and folded his bedding, I could predict that he was going to be throwing his belongings outside the cell quite soon. The men pulled this sort of prank when they were especially angry or edgy; hurling bedding, shelves, or the wooden plugs that supported them was a way to vent their anger. Or they might tear up the springs of their beds. Each of the furnishings that an inmate destroyed cost him twenty dollars, which was drawn from pay he received for work in the industries.

More than once, Anna and I would be hosting a dinner party for our colleagues, especially my buddy Bill Long and his wife Jean, and I'd get a call telling me that "So-and-so is tearing up his cell." Both Bill and I would leave and take care of it. Anna and Jean learned to keep meals warm for us.

Spreading the Word

Prisoners tried to communicate with each other by passing notes through the bars. The folded message might be labeled "Carry this down to cell 12." An inmate who was asked to pass notes from the cell next door to somebody down the line was sometimes annoyed by the interruption, and may even have declined to help, but usually, he cooperated.

This underground messaging system was, of course, forbidden. The guards were on the lookout for notes being passed—an arm extending beyond the bars of a cell was a good tip-off—and would confiscate the communication. These messages often conveyed news of escape plans or other information the prisoners wanted to share without being seen talking. So when authorities intercepted one of these notes, they got a good peek at what the prisoners were cooking up.

Inmates also communicated in other ways. When they heard someone entering through the main door of the cellhouse, an array of shaving mirrors would flash along the corridors as they tried to determine who it might be. They would also use hoots and birdcalls to alert their fellow inmates that an officer was nearby.

Entertainment

In 1955, the year before I came on staff, each cell was outfitted with a radio and headset. The radio had only two channels, but, considering that they had nothing like it before, it must've seemed like a luxury. Over these channels, the men could listen to sports events or music. When there was trouble in the prison, the control tower turned the broadcast off.

There was also a library. Convicts could not access it in person. Instead, they were given a list of books and magazines and from that list, made requests. A cart came around the cellblocks weekly to deliver and take back books. There were no newspapers.

Sometimes, the inmate who brought books was also delivering

contraband. For example, a piece of metal that someone was working on to make a knife or some other item would come along with the reading material. Once, one of the cell-bound convicts snitched on a library inmate, telling a guard, "Watch him; he's got something in that cart." The library inmate went to the hole for that. It's funny to look back now and see how much interaction there was between convicts and guards. To an outsider, it seemed like inmates could rarely talk to each other, much less to the guards. However, this was far from true.

Isolation

D Block, or isolation, was the prison's confinement area for those who had committed serious violations of institution rules, were uncontrollable, or had attacked an inmate or an officer. In isolation, cells were organized in three tiers just as they were for B and C Blocks. But the only way correctional officers could enter D Block was to signal the officer up in the gun gallery, who controlled the doors for that unit.

Prisoners who had committed crimes while serving their sentences were sent to segregation, which had two classes of isolation confinement: thirty-six single-door cells, and six double-door cells; the latter were familiarly referred to as "the Hole." In the six double-door cells, one of the doors was solid, which cut off the light.

D Block's cells all faced an exterior wall with huge barred windows, and those in the single-door cells had the benefit of the light that streamed in through them. These cells were constructed similarly to those in B and C Blocks, but prisoners in segregation did not leave their cells for meals, recreation, or work. Typically, an inmate was incarcerated in D Block for only a few days. Robert Stroud (AZ-594), the so-called Bird Man of Alcatraz, was the only permanent resident in this section; Stroud, by the way, bore no resemblance to Burt Lancaster, either physically or in his demeanor. Lancaster, who played the title role in the movie *Birdman of Alcatraz*, was a far more sympathetic soul than the man in our prison.

Not everybody in isolation could enjoy the sunshine, as the shit-slinging prisoner I met on my first day found out. The truly agonizing punishment was to be put in extreme isolation—one of the six closed cells. Sealed in by a solid metal exterior door and a barred interior door, the prisoner remained in darkness without furniture, heat, or a wash basin. A mattress was tossed in the cell in the evening and removed in the morning; during the day, the inmate sat in the dark on a hard, cold floor. Meager meals were served twice a day.

One particular cell was reserved for extraordinarily dangerous or suicidal prisoners. A man sentenced to serve time in this cell was stripped naked, and the only amenity he had was a toilet, which was set level with the floor's surface to prevent it from being broken.

The outer doors on these closed cells each had a peephole so the guards could do their counting and inspect the interior of the cell without entering it. Using his flashlight, the guard would peer into the cell to locate the inmate and confirm that he was alive. As a guard surveyed the interior with this beam of light, the prisoner naturally squinted right into it at first, reacted to the light, and then scurried away. However, sometimes the prisoner anticipated the flashlight and played dead. This ruse would create an uproar and win the prisoner some attention, for which he could hardly be punished any more than he already was.

Kitchen and Dining Hall

Except for those in isolation, prisoners were released from their cells and led to the dining hall three times a day. The food was presented cafeteria style and the men lined up and selected what they wanted to eat; they could take as much food as they wanted and were expected to eat all they took. The kitchen was behind the dining hall. Both areas were kept spotless, and the floors were polished. Under supervision, prisoners worked in the kitchen and the dining hall, cooking and serving.

A dining hall serving two hundred or more meals at a time can be a place for mischief, even if those who were using it weren't tough criminals. This was one of only two places (the rec yard was the other) where prisoners could congregate, and human nature was evident everywhere. The men sat at long tables, five to a side, and were allowed to talk. In the early days of the prison, during Warden James Johnston's tenure, there was a strict rule of silence, which applied to mealtimes as well, but that rule was long gone by the time I arrived. While I served at Alcatraz, the ten-man tables were replaced with tables that only seated four. It was unfortunate, because the new arrangement promoted cliques and more ill will among the men.

I'll never forget Lieutenant Jack Mitchell, who was pretty obese but very agile. Once, while supervising the dining hall, he detected an argument between two of the prisoners, and jumped to intervene in the confrontation. However, he slipped on the highly polished floor and went flying into the air. The prisoners quickly got out of his way, but Mitchell couldn't stop. He landed spread-eagle on a dining table, sending steel trays, plates, and food flying. Not the kind of man to be embarrassed, he just got up and dusted the food off his uniform. None of the men said anything; they were a bit afraid of him.

Many of these men were used to hard living and hard liquor and craved a bit of hooch from time to time. This led to their frequent clandestine attempts to make a concoction referred to as raisin jack, or pruno. Various schemes were devised to distill alcohol from raisins, peaches, or anything that would ferment. Sometimes, they would even make it in a garden hose, stuffing the hose with fruit and a little sugar and then letting the mixture rest until it packed a wallop.

According to Bill Long, who did several tours of duty in the kitchen, the bakery behind the kitchen was the center for moonshine antics. One of the officers who supervised the cooking of meals had quite a nose, according to Bill. In one instance, he was convinced brewing was going on, and he started patrolling for the source of the scent. For several days, he searched from corner to corner. Finally, one afternoon, he strolled by the fire extinguisher hanging on the wall, and stopped. That's where he found the hidden mini-still.

The Dangers of Spontaneity

There were instances when prisoners did not really misbehave, but they forgot where they were. An inmate working down on the dock began to stare at one of the female residents, who was walking on an incline above the dock. This woman, no doubt the wife of an employee, was very well endowed. Without thinking, he whistled at her. He was immediately arrested and taken to the hole. And he lost his prized job on the dock.

While it may seem a severe punishment, prisoners were constantly instructed not to make any gestures or approaches to residents. They were told that repeatedly. No doubt this man thought an appreciative whistle wasn't so very serious. More likely, he wasn't thinking at all.

In another episode, which took place on a very hot day, I

was working outside with a crew of prisoners building a square concrete tank destined to hold about 200,000 gallons of diesel oil for the generator. It was probably eight to ten feet high, but set below grade, so that the top was level with the ground; at this point in the construction, it was basically a big ditch, and it was filled with water. Suddenly, one of my crew ditched his clothes and dove in, then paddled around the newly dug tank. This convict had thrown off his shirt and pants so fast, I couldn't believe it. He had probably been planning to dive in while we were working on the tank. I'm sure it wasn't just the intense heat that inspired him. At any rate, I told him to get out, and he did. He said, "Mr. Mahoney, I don't care if I'm going to the hole. I just wanted to take a quick swim."

Instead of sending him to the hole, I imposed a different kind of punishment. I said to him, "You really embarrassed me." Embarrassing a correctional officer was a consequence most prisoners wanted to avoid. I couldn't bring myself to have him sent to the hole over this; the exercise the men got in the yard could not compare with the facilities and experiences they enjoyed before they were imprisoned. Of course, his "heroic exploit" was the subject of much talk and envy among the other inmates for quite some time.

A Visit from the Judge

One time, a federal judge notified the warden that he was coming to visit Alcatraz with his secretary and was going to take a look in the cellhouse. He didn't ask for permission from the BOP, and he didn't mention that his secretary was a woman.

We locked everyone up before he entered the cellhouse, and he and his secretary walked along the corridors. He had sentenced half the convicts there, and talked to them like they were old buddies.

They answered, "Your Honor," or "I'm working on my case." And he would say, "Well, I'm glad to hear that."

His secretary was a good-looking gal, almost a Hollywood type, and she was certainly knowledgeable. I heard her talking with the judge, and she recalled many details of the cases in question. We never let women in the cellhouse, so her presence was highly unusual; the only reason she was there was because the judge strode in with her without obtaining clearance. But the convicts behaved themselves. Had there been any disrespect, the offenders would have gone straight to the hole.

Taming Violence

Men who were sent to Alcatraz had proven themselves to be incorrigible at other penitentiaries. They had been convicted of federal crimes like bank robbery, murder, racketeering, kidnapping, and even spying. When the Bureau of Prisons established staffing levels at Alcatraz, they kept this in mind. Whereas most federal penitentiaries assigned one guard for every dozen prisoners, at Alcatraz, the ratio was one to three.

These men, who had harmed society while free, brought their warped interactions with them to the Rock. Prisoners struck out at each other when they perceived rivalry, humiliations, or persecution. Certainly, the other source of frustration was that they were each distinct individuals locked in identical cells with few outlets for expressing their urges or defusing aggression. Their beds had steel frames that were not attached to the floor. Occasionally, a prisoner would pick up the end of his bed and let it drop. Repeatedly. This was especially effective during the middle of the night, when the sound radiated throughout the prison building and as far down as the dock.

Work life for correctional officers was a mixture of long spans of routine security management interspersed with moments of high stress when containing violence or preventing escape attempts. I learned what I was facing on my second day on the job, when I was assigned to stand guard in the kitchen. Suddenly, several correctional officers tore into the kitchen, dashed into the dishwashing room, and pulled out an inmate who had been mauled with a lead pipe. His head had been split open like a cracked egg. It was a gruesome and bloody sight. They laid him, unconscious, over the threshold to the main kitchen, which was the most convenient position for the medics to attend to him. I had to step over him, and as I did so, I looked down at this ghastly spectacle and wondered if he would survive. He lasted long enough to be shipped to the medical facility in Springfield.

Most security measures were designed into the structure of the prison building itself, but others involved the behavior of guards. To prevent a convict from wresting control of a firearm from an officer, all guards were unarmed unless they were stationed in the gun gallery. (Though it was illegal for correctional officers to use them, some guards carried saps—leather-encased lead weights, molded to fit the hand—for protection.) In extreme situations, when guards needed to use firearms, they had to stand at least twenty feet away from inmates.

We took many measures—both large and small—to ensure that no object could easily be used as a weapon For example, in the "small" category, all prisoners' shoes were reconstructed, replacing metal nails and staples with wood.

Blades

Since stabbings were the most common form of violence among the prisoners, the legitimate use of scissors, knives, and razors required special attention.

Scissors

Scissors were locked in various cabinets throughout the prison where they might be needed—for instance, in the clothing room, where prisoners' uniforms were maintained and distributed, or in one of the several factories that the prison operated. In the factories, industrial-sized scissors, with blades almost a foot long, were essential tools. Each inmate with an authorized need for a pair of scissors had to sign them out, and a record was kept of when he returned them. All scissors were stored in the same locked cabinet, to which I had the key. Depending on what job the convict was performing, the correctional officer in charge decided whether his request was legitimate. It was not my job to work in the clothing factory but for a time, I had the duty to issue scissors. While I did this, other correctional officers stood outside, checking inmates who were coming into the factory to work.

Alcatraz prisoners made hundreds of thousands of uniforms for use by various divisions of the government. They used automatic fabric cutters to punch through dozens of layers of fabric at a time. But then they needed to make those cuts more precise, trimming the edges with handheld scissors.

One day as I was issuing scissors, an inmate approached and said he needed "the big ones," which I gave him. All of a sudden, three of my prisoner crew (all of whom had scissors) started flailing at each other. Two held up short scissors but one had the industrial-sized blades I had just issued him. He rammed them into another inmate's chest so far that the long blades came out the man's back, and blood sprayed everywhere.

Just as I rushed him, the perpetrator slashed another man in the wrist repeatedly; when I went to grab the victim, his hand almost came off in my hands. The doctor later told me that it was a wonder the man's hand didn't fall off entirely. The third inmate had non-lethal stab wounds in the arms and chest. I was unarmed and dealing with all three of them at once; though I was not their target, I was in the way of their attempts to kill one another. No other staff members were around to witness or help me.

I struggled alone, and finally, the rest of the convict crew came to my aid, grabbing the three men. Coming to the aid of a correctional officer was unheard-of, absolutely taboo within the convict culture. It was considered dishonorable. I can only attribute their help to my good reputation among them. Also, convicts normally went to great lengths to avoid injuring a staff member because they didn't want to end up in the hole.

Two convicts grabbed hold of the one who had been stabbed in the chest; locking arms and forming a kind of cradle, they carried him up to the hospital. Amazingly, this man recuperated in Alcatraz's hospital and survived.

The one whose wrist was badly mangled groaned, "God damn, my hand hurts." His hand was saved, but he was disabled from then on. The only small saving grace was that he was right-handed and it was his left hand that had been mutilated. I felt terrible about having grabbed him by the wrist, but he didn't blame me.

When I got home, I told Anna what had happened; my son, Steve, who was about six at the time, was listening in. Steve wanted to hear the details, and I told him just the way I described it here. Steve then asked why the one convict stabbed the other, and I had to say that I really didn't know. "They just didn't like each other, Steve," I said. Although my family was very protected physically, occasionally they came to know some of the grim details of my work. I couldn't protect them totally from that.

Most children on the island were very curious about what transpired behind the prison's walls. But they were not allowed to even approach the main door, much less enter the building, so their curiosity usually went unsatisfied.

Knives

One of my duties in the kitchen was to issue the knives from the knife cabinet. When a convict needed a butcher knife because he was assigned to butcher meat, we recorded his name and number and the type of knife he was issued. Generally, several knives were in use when convicts were preparing meals, cutting up vegetables, and the like.

During the seven years I worked at the prison, no knife issued from the kitchen was ever used for an assault on another inmate. There was some honor about that, which the inmates never violated. (It's a pity they didn't feel the same way about scissors.) The correctional officers in charge of knives were always able to account for every one of them.

However, homemade knives were a different story. When they wanted a deadly weapon, inmates devised their own implements. They would generally seize upon a piece of metal found during their duties or in the factories and sharpen it against the concrete in their cells.

Stabbings were most common in the shower and clothing rooms. To take a shower, a prisoner first had to turn in his dirty clothes to the clothing room, and during this time, he was naked and vulnerable. Ronald Simcox (AZ-1131) knifed another convict in the shower and was charged with attempted murder. His defense attorney alleged that the man Simcox attacked (whose nickname was Dog Man) originally had the knife and that Simcox took it away from him and stabbed him in an act of self-defense.

During the trial, the prosecutor asked, "How could he take the knife from another man?"

The defense attorney instructed Simcox to remove his shirt. Built like Charles Atlas, this prisoner worked out in his cell regularly, doing push-ups, handstands, and other displays of muscle. The exhibition of Simcox's physique convinced the jury (many of whom were women) that he was capable of wresting a knife from an opponent.

Simcox was deadly. He'd killed inmates on Alcatraz and spent many a week locked up in D Block. An experienced murderer, he would lecture fellow inmates on ways to kill people. Among his pieces of advice was this warped pearl of wisdom: "When you push the knife in, you've got to twist it. If you don't twist it, they can sew it up."

Razors

Just as with scissors and knives, issuing razor blades was a balancing act. Since inmates were required to shave, razors were necessary, but blades needed to be strictly controlled. Each inmate was provided with a single-blade safety razor. When the blade became dull, the inmate would put it on the grill of his cell door and an officer would replace it with a new one. The exchanges were carefully monitored, as stockpiling was to be avoided at all costs.

Curiously, those convicts who chose to cut or stab people never used razors—except for one sickening incident perpetrated by the lethal Simcox, who was quite persuasive. He convinced several convicts that they could get publicity and claim prison brutality by cutting their Achilles tendons with their razors.

"You're going to get all kinds of recognition this way," he assured them.

Although he was convinced that his scheme—mutilation for glorification—would work, Simcox did not maim himself. He was proud of his physique and took care of it.

Ten or twelve prisoners used their razors to slash the back of their ankles. Some were lucky; they didn't cut deeply enough to injure themselves permanently. But others managed to sever their tendons. To their despair, neither publicity nor notoriety followed their deeds, just life with a handicap.

When we first encountered these injuries, Tom Reeves, the medical technical assistant (MTA), bandaged them. The inmates simply removed the bandages and cut themselves again. Then he put casts on them to prevent further injury. This was frustrating for correctional officers and our superiors, since we knew what they meant to achieve and how they had been duped into crippling themselves permanently.

Years later, when I was working in the federal prison in Marion, Illinois, I met some of these convicts again. The balls of their feet collapsed with each step, flapping as they walked. It was a pitiful sight. One of them told me how sorry he was that he ever followed Simcox's advice.

Matches

Convicts were given a weekly allotment of two packs of Wings cigarettes, the very cheapest kind. Sometimes, they started fires in their cells with the matches that accompanied their cigarettes. They even made small firecrackers by scratching off the powder from several match heads until they had a tiny pile. Then they would wrap the material in toilet paper, fashion a fuse, and throw it against their cell wall, making a heck of a racket.

One prisoner set his mattress on fire. Bill Long and I couldn't get into his cell to douse the flames because he had stuffed clothing into the cell door in such a way that it was jammed shut. Meanwhile, the inmate was on his hands and knees blowing on the flame in his mattress to stoke it. Bill tried to get his attention, but could not.

When eventually we were able to open the door, Bill threw two buckets of water on the convict. Each time Bill aimed at him, the inmate turned his back so that he could keep his little bonfire burning. The mattress was destroyed and the convict went to the hole.

Suicides

Suicides and suicide attempts were very rare, mostly because we checked and rechecked prisoners in their cells so frequently. But they did happen from time to time. It seems the attempts were often motivated not by events within the prison, but by relationships outside. If an inmate received a discouraging letter from home, something that indicated that a relationship had no future, for example, it would upset the man greatly.

Usually, a despondent convict would try to hang himself by tying a sheet to the bars. More often than not, an officer on his count would discover the individual hanging and would be able to cut him down in time to save his life. But the success rate was not 100 percent.

As soon as we detected a suicide attempt, we immediately took the inmate into the infirmary and initiated procedures that got all other convicts back into their cells.

The man who tried to kill himself would get immediate medical and psychiatric attention to see what damage he had inflicted. Then he would be sent to an open-front cell in isolation under twenty-four-hour supervision. In my experience, no inmate made a second attempt to kill himself.

The Dangerous, the Incorrigible, and the Merely Outrageous

The little inmate society that the federal Bureau of Prisons assembled on Alcatraz was a pressure cooker in which distressed individuals had to learn to adapt to and cope with one another. Inmates often called Alcatraz "Hoover's Heaven" after FBI chief J. Edgar Hoover, which perhaps reflected their feelings of victimization. Even under strict administrative regulation and supervision, they were still able to create their own social order.

The prisoners used several forms of currency, cigarettes most often. For instance, on the night they were served steak in the dining hall, someone might swap a pack of cigarettes for someone else's slab of beef.

Laundry care offered another opportunity to barter. If a prisoner worked in the laundry and owed another prisoner a favor, he might repay him by giving his clothes—which could be identified by the inmate number stamped on them—extra care during ironing and folding.

While you hear of honor among thieves, in Alcatraz, their culture was a network of resentments. If an inmate told prison officers of the misdeeds of another inmate, he was marked for life; ratting was a sure way to get dead fast. The man who informed knew he was marked, and usually asked prison authorities to transfer him to a safe environment, which meant a long stretch in the isolation ward.

Although inmates were under extremely close supervision and housed singly in separate cells, they could still pose a threat to one another. Convicts had contact with one another on the way to and from meals, at their tables, in the showers, and at their workstations. That's where they were most at risk.

Keeping Men Inside

"Under lock and key" is the common term for enforced security. Correctional officers had to learn and implement the system for keeping locks and keys safe and under control. The prison control center, or armory, stored the weapons that correctional officers might need in an emergency. Otherwise, as mentioned, we worked throughout the prison and fulfilled our duties unarmed.

However, the use of keys and access to them were central to our effectiveness. When an officer required a key, its issuance was recorded. The officer who held these keys could open anything, from the cellhouse to the doors to the recreation yard, kitchen, and hospital. Some keys were highly restricted, and the officers' captain was the only one who could authorize their use. This was especially true of the keys to the clothing and supply rooms.

Despite the elaborate mechanisms and routines devised for controlling cell doors, some prisoners found ways to undermine them. Once in awhile, an inmate would get a piece of wood—perhaps a fragment of a handle from the broom shop—and lodge it in a way that kept the door to his cell from opening. Most often, this was done when an inmate wanted to start a fire in his cell and didn't want officers to extinguish it. Why would a man want to start a fire in his cell? Possibly because he was angry and wanted to bring attention to himself. Such displays infuriated the other convicts. "Here I am, doing time, sucker, and now I can hardly breathe," I heard one man say. Inmates would happily batter one another for that.

Bill Long remembered incidents like this as well. Bill and his wife lived on the floor just above us in the early days while we were still in Building 64. The internal phone—the one that connected employees to one another' s apartments—was just outside his door. One night, Anna and I were having dinner with Bill and Jean at their apartment. The phone rang and Bill went out to answer it. When he returned he said, "There's trouble up top, and we've got to go."

"Up top" meant the prison. When we got there, we quickly discovered the source of the trouble. Sam Tiblow (AZ-1265) was ripping up the furnishings in his cell, burning them, and throwing them out. As we got closer, we saw that Tiblow had broken the toilet, and water was gushing out of the cell. He was also hollering and making a ruckus. He smashed his guitar on the bars and then threw it out in bits and pieces. That guitar had been one of his prized possessions.

Sam was furious because he had recently received a disciplinary report. It appears he had an argument with an officer, who reported the incident, and Sam felt that the report was unjust. He assumed he was going to the hole, and since that was the case, he figured he'd go for a valid reason: burning down his cell.

The cells on the second and third tiers were fronted by a walkway with a railing; the officers patrolled along this walkway. Our dinner parties were always dress-up affairs, so we were in our best duds. Bill placed one leg over the rail to protect his good suit from the water pouring out of Sam's cell.

Then he hollered out, "Sam! What's going on?"

Sam, who recognized his voice, griped about getting a "bum rap."

Bill reasoned with him: "You know you're going to the hole, Sam. I've got my good evening clothes on and a new pair of shoes. I don't want to get them all wet in that damn water. I don't want to have to come in there and wrestle with you. You know we're going to take you in, so why don't we just go easily?"

Bill promised Sam that not a hand would be laid on him. "But if we have to pull you out of the cell, you're liable to get a little injured," he warned.

Bill was not threatening him with violence as much as he was predicting the likely outcome of resistance. Tentatively, Sam came out, reminding Bill of his promise not to touch him. "Nobody's going to touch you, Sam. I'll walk with you," my partner assured him. Sam behaved like a gentleman as we walked him to isolation. After this short burst of excitement, Bill and I went back down the hill and finished supper with our wives.

Relationships with Prisoners

The relationship between prisoners and their guardians, the correctional officers, is a topic that could fill a shelf. It's a common belief that prison guards manipulate and even brutalize prisoners in many ways, and the job certainly provides opportunities for cruelty if one is wired that way.

At Alcatraz, a lot of interplay between the inmates and guards was positive. The convicts were, of course, extremely dangerous, but they were more dangerous to each other than they were to us. No prisoner assaulted a staff member while I was there.

Cruelty to prisoners was definitely not my style. Some confrontations with prisoners forced us to get physical, but my aim was always to calm the prisoner down and never overdo. If he became physical with a correctional officer, the prisoner knew he was going into the hole. This in itself often cooled resistance.

I had been a very competent amateur boxer and was confident of my power and technique. Sometimes I would tell a convict, "If you want to fight with somebody, check with me. You won't win, but at least you can give it a whirl. I just don't lose." I was quite large and had very large, meaty hands, so I think convicts could see that it would be difficult for them if we got in a fight.

It wasn't in my character to beat anybody up; I would not mistreat someone who couldn't defend himself. But there were officers who simply wanted to thump people. I occasionally had to appeal to colleagues to restrain themselves from abusing our charges. Some of them just wouldn't listen; they persisted in mistreating the men and eventually, were fired.

Once, a correctional officer used a sap to strike Joe Wagstaff (AZ-1072, more about him later), and he wouldn't let up. I restrained him, saying, "No, no! You're going to kill him! Stop!" We were to use force only in extreme situations, and this was not an extreme circumstance. But that correctional officer was a wild man anyway. They called him "the Arizona wildcat"; he was always in trouble but rarely disciplined.

Dealing with the diverse personalities I encountered in prison work—both the convicts and my colleagues—was key to the satisfaction my job gave me. I felt it was my task to persuade a certain kind of personality to come around, blend in, and behave. I like to believe that the prisoners understood me. They knew I respected them and that I was honest. Some prisoners would occasionally try to bribe officers so they could get a particular product or a service, but

I heard convicts say to one another, "No, don't try to bribe Mahoney, because he's honest. You're not going to get anything out of him, and you're just going to go to the hole."

I wasn't unique. While it may have been true at other prisons that correctional officers had adversarial relationships with the prisoners, this was not my perception of Alcatraz. By and large, officers and prisoners treated each other decently.

Michael Esslinger, in his book, *Alcatraz: A Definitive History of the Penitentiary Years,* quotes former inmate William Radkay saying he considered that the majority of staff treated inmates respectfully, and inmates appreciated that, even while conversation with officers was limited. From my point of view, I'd have to agree.

This mindset was largely the result of the leadership of Warden Paul Madigan, a jewel of a superior as far as I was concerned. A well-educated, distinguished man of integrity, Madigan was frequently invited to speak at public functions. He brought honor to our penitentiary on the island.

The Man Called "Promising Paul"

Warden Madigan was also a good mentor when it came to dealing with prisoners. While he opposed cruelty, he told us to be firm.

"Don't get upset when you have to address inmates, or even shake them down," he told me once. He was referring to instances when we had to question the prisoner and make a report on their actions. By "shaking them down," he meant frisking them for knives or other contraband. "They have very thick skins. These guys have been through an awful lot in their lives, and they will act as though they're really upset over the way you approach them. But they have had worse done to them hundreds of times," Madigan assured me.

I've seen prisoners try to implicate a correctional officer who was disciplining or frisking him. If the officer had to check between the prisoner's legs for a knife or contraband, the prisoner might protest, "Oh please, officer, don't do that to me, I can't stand it."

Madigan warned me, "Don't let them pull that on you."

Sometimes, I had to train new correctional officers on how to frisk a prisoner. If the convict wailed that he was being harassed—trying to measure how much he could manipulate the new recruit—I would warn the convict: "Knock it off and knock it off right now."

"Yes, Mr. Mahoney," was the usual response. The prisoner knew that I was telling him not to undermine or try to deceive the new officer. This is just part of the psychology of dealing with people who are incarcerated.

A natural Irishman, Warden Madigan got along with everyone, although an occasional disappointed employee called him by his nickname, "Promising Paul." I asked him about this label, and he explained where it came from. "There are times when, for example, I cannot get an employee moved to the housing where he would like to live. Sometimes it's better to promise I will move him even though I may not be able to fulfill that promise in the near future. My job is to find employees and keep them. That disappointed one would probably leave anyway."

The Troubled Prisoner

If a prisoner was psychotic, it was a challenge to convince him to cooperate. It could be equally difficult to persuade other correctional officers that the prisoner's problem was mental.

Convicts won't always seek help. Often we tried to soothe a man by assuring him, "I'm going to try and get you some help." Frequently, the response would be, "I don't need any help." In such cases, I usually just kept talking, trying to get the man to a psychiatrist. It was my way of giving service and the way I wanted to do my job.

The Alcatraz infirmary, which we called the hospital, tended to the illnesses and sometimes the wounds prisoners suffered. On one occasion, I was assigned to retrieve a prisoner from isolation and take him there for an interview with a psychiatrist. Another officer and I stood next to the convict as he discussed his problems with the psychiatrist. At one point, the inmate showed the doctor the lines on his palms and the doctor responded by showing his own. They were sitting with their hands extended to each other as they calmly discussed their palm lines.

Abruptly, the convict grabbed the doctor's hand and bit his thumb and index finger. Blood spurted everywhere, and the poor psychiatrist yelped like a dog. But he appealed to us: "I don't want him to suffer any repercussions for this. He was just venting his anger." Nonetheless, we escorted the prisoner back to isolation and put him in the dark cell, whereas previously he was lodged in an open-front cell. Later, that same prisoner requested another session with a psychiatrist. A different doctor was summoned, but refused to interview him because he thought the man was too dangerous.

The Missing Sleeve

Because we were dealing with incarcerated men, violent incidents arose from time to time. In the case of my buddy, Bill Long, the violence was inflicted on his uniform. The BOP issued officers uniforms about every two years. At one point, Bill requisitioned a new one. "And it took a long time to get it, too," he recalled. I remember how proud he was to put it on when it finally arrived. When time came for those official duds to be cleaned, Bill sent the uniform to the laundry. It came back minus a sleeve.

"Somebody cut my sleeve off. I imagine they'd like to have had my arm in it," he reckoned. Bill couldn't think of anyone among the ten or so prisoners working in the laundry who held a grudge against him. He asked some laundry workers what they knew about the incident, but nobody would talk.

Burlap Suit

It was rare for an inmate to get to the point of being released at Alcatraz. Most were serving very long, or even multiple, sentences, many for life. But I recall an occasion when an inmate did make it to his release date. A few inmates who worked in the tailor shop sewing clothing for the military gathered pieces from burlap bags, then made him a suit they felt was fitting for a man going back to the outside world. Though our rules would not have allowed this "suit" to be made, it was a small gesture, and one I found both funny and touching.

Characters and Their Nicknames

To our faces, the inmates called us "sir" or addressed us by Mr. and our surnames. But privately, they had their own handles for us. They called me "P. T." for my initials. "Professor" was their name for Bill Long because he had a college education. Lieutenant Lloyd Miller was dubbed "Blue Boy." A very heavy man, he turned blue in the face at the least exertion.

The names they used for each other were far more colorful and rooted in histories few of us could fathom. But they were so pervasive and embedded that we officers used them too, though it was certainly against protocol. Bumpy, the Green Lizard, Pork Chops, Dog Man, and Spider were among the more vivid ones. They were so commonly used that I could not always remember the men's real names. And then, of course, there was Robert Stroud, the "Birdman."

Bumpy Johnson

Bumpy Johnson (AZ-1117), an African-American, was involved with an organized crime group known as Murder, Inc., or the Brownsville Boys, in New York. His given name was Ellsworth. I presumed he earned the nickname Bumpy by being whacked on the head a few times. I never knew his real name until years after the prison closed. He served a respectable stretch of time at Alcatraz, then was sent to USP Atlanta, Georgia.

He strongly objected to the food there. He said he told the prison officials in Atlanta, "This slop isn't fit for man or beast. You can ship me back to Alcatraz." That's just what they did, and he was happy. That's how good our food was. We would sometimes go fishing in the bay and bring back our catch to add to dinners for inmates; Dungeness crabs and striped bass were popular. This free supplement was one of the few nice additions to their otherwise quiet and boring existence in their cells.

The Green Lizard

I never knew how the Green Lizard came by this handle, but one of his capers that at first seemed comical turned tragic. Every year, the inmates set up and decorated a Christmas tree in the dining hall, as was the tradition. One Christmas, the Green Lizard leapt up and wrapped his arms around the tree, then whisked it from the dining hall, leaving ornaments and tinsel in his wake. It was an unusual prank, and few appreciated this travesty of a Christmas ritual. He spent the holiday in the hole.

Even though he must have known what the punishment would be, the next Christmas, the Lizard pulled the same trick. Boughs were breaking, lights were in disarray, and ornaments were crushed.

Although Bill had him adequately restrained, one of the guards needlessly clubbed the Lizard over the head with a sap in front of all the inmates in the dining hall. It was obvious that the Green Lizard was headed for the hole for absconding with the tree, which was itself destroyed in the process. The inmates who had witnessed the drama resented the guard's unnecessary abuse in using a sap.

Within the month, the convicts chose the deadly Wagstaff to take revenge. He prepared himself with a homemade knife. Later, in the dining hall, Wagstaff advanced toward the officer who disciplined the Green Lizard, but in his path he encountered inmate Jim Gilliam (AZ-1361).

Now, Wagstaff had also had a beef against Gilliam, who was working under me serving food in the mess hall. As I heard it, Wagstaff and his cronies thought Gilliam was working far too diligently, and they wanted him to slow down the pace. (Gilliam's habit of shouting at the other inmates and saying that when he got out, he'd go after their wives and daughters also made him many enemies.) So Gilliam was on Wagstaff's hit list. At the moment of the attack, Gilliam, who was carrying a tray of soft ice cream or milk, intercepted Wagstaff. Wagstaff lunged and stabbed him, and the white, slippery food went flying. Bill Long took Wagstaff down, grabbing both him and his knife. But poor Bill slipped on the floor and couldn't right himself. My buddy called out, "Help me, help me." He had his foot on Wagstaff's wrist, but he couldn't wrench the knife away. The other correctional officers ran to help, but they also slipped and slid. Finally, enough officers were able to make it across the floor to disarm Wagstaff.

Fortunately for Gilliam, his ribs kept the knife from penetrating too deeply and saved his life. Later, when I went to visit Gilliam in the Alcatraz infirmary, he said, "I've got to get to Jerry because he's the one who done this to me."

He was referring to Jerry Clymore (AZ-1339), whom he felt was the instigator of the plot and the one who had put the contract out on the correctional officer who thumped Wagstaff.

"Have you talked to the associate warden about this?" I asked.

He said he had. I too tried to impress on the associate warden the gravity of the situation. Some days later, Gilliam and Clymore were both in the shower, and Clymore stabbed Gilliam in the back. The blade was so thin that it curved around Gilliam's spine. It didn't kill him, but it disabled him for life.

Clymore was eventually tried in federal court for attempted murder, and I was among the witnesses. Under prodding from the defense attorney, the correctional officer who removed the blade from Gilliam's back testified on the stand that it was possible that, in trying to remove the knife from Gilliam's body, he might have pushed it in a mite more.

As soon as he said that, I knew that we had lost the case. The officer's statement led the jury to conclude that that single subtle maneuver was enough to exonerate Wagstaff. There was no conviction.

However, Clymore went to the hole for a long time. They sent Gilliam to US Medical Center for Federal Prisoners in Springfield for physical analysis and later on, to USP Marion, Illinois, the institution that replaced Alcatraz when it closed in 1963.

Years later, when I was working at USP Marion, I met up with

Gilliam. He wanted to work for me again, but I was overseeing heavy construction jobs and I realized he simply could not physically handle the tasks. I couldn't hire him, and it broke my heart.

All of these events flowed from the theft of the Christmas tree.

Lethal Wagstaff

As for the murderous Wagstaff, I had several run-ins with him. He always seemed to target me for his venom. On one occasion, filling in for another officer, I was working the gun gallery. The officer in that position was the only one in the cellhouse who had a weapon—a gas gun, a rifle-like instrument that spewed tear gas. From the gallery, I was protected in an enclosed area and had control over opening and closing the cells in D Block, that is, isolation.

Wagstaff was quartered in isolation and I could see from my station that he was having a confrontation with an officer. Wagstaff knew that I was observing and writing the argument down as I was hearing it. He knew the consequences of my report could be incarceration in a closed-door cell. He looked up at me in the gun gallery, and he said, "Look, you cheese-eatin' … you Irish cheese-eatin' sonofabitch, I can kill you."

There was no way to punish him for this insolence beyond the punishment he was already receiving, so I just let it go.

Pork Chops

This inmate lived up to his name. Always hungry, Pork Chops was a fat little toad who stole food at the least provocation. He was mischievous and went to the hole many times.

The poor man was often the unfortunate dupe of inmates who convinced him that he was losing lucrative television and radio appearances by virtue of being on Alcatraz. Famous prisoners urged him to sue the Bureau of Prisons and make a lot of money. He tried this several times, but not surprisingly, the cases were always thrown out of federal court.

Blackie Audett

Theodore "Blackie" Audett (AZ-208, -551, and -1217) was a pleasure to be around. It may seem curious to praise men whom you know are among the worst in society, but for whatever reason, goodness shone through some of them. Blackie had done well over fifty years in prison for bank robberies, but he never pulled a job in his home state of Oregon. I once asked him why not, and he said, "Naw, Mr. Mahoney, I couldn't do that. That's my home state." So he had some kind of value system, it appears, even if it was only geographical.

He was a terrific listener, or maybe eavesdropper is a better word. He could pick up conversations from twenty feet. Blackie's ears perked up when he approached the officers' dining hall. At one point, he overheard Warden Madigan discussing his intention to promote a certain officer. The warden was eager to tell the officer personally, but Blackie got to him first: "Don't tell anyone, but you got your promotion."

He did that not once, but several times, beating Madigan with news the warden intended to announce himself. Madigan was furious when he found out the soon-to-be lieutenant already knew. He sputtered with mock seriousness, "I'm going to put Audett in the hole. That SOB is taking my job away from me."

Blackie got along with both his fellow convicts and the staff. In one instance, he was carrying food on a cart through the cell house to the officers' dining hall. Another inmate, driven by God knows what, assaulted Blackie. Both the staff and the other convicts jumped in and worked this individual over for attacking Blackie. Naturally, that convict wound up in the hole.

Spider

Spider got his nickname from an antic he liked to pull during the prisoner count. He had very powerful hands, mighty enough that he could hold himself up near the top of the cell—like Spiderman—eluding the correctional officers as they came around.

When the officers didn't see anyone inside the cell, they took off to alert their superiors and organize a search. When they came back and found him in his cell, they'd throw him in the hole.

He knew what he was in for, but seemed willing to take the risk. Plus, they didn't keep him in isolation too long. He'd be advised to "knock it off," but he'd do it again anyway.

Teddy Green

This was not Teddy Green's real name, and how he came to be entered in the prison roster with it (Theodore Green, AZ-1180) was a mystery to me. Teddy told me he had been involved in a Brink's robbery, referring to the security company that transported money for banks and the government. He showed me pictures of himself in a tuxedo in a swank club in New York, and another in Boston.

"Let me tell you, Mr. Mahoney, I lived high," he said. "I'm paying for it."

Wild Bill

While a pleasant and humorous character, this African-American prisoner was also unpredictable, and he created trouble more than once. It was his job to drive the forklift down by the dock. Every so often, he would drive like a maniac. Once he drove it too close to the bay, and it spilled over the bank and crashed onto the rocks near the water. Wild Bill got scratched up, but nothing more. As for the forklift, we needed a crane to retrieve it in less-than-usable condition.

One weekend, Wild Bill was having an argument with another inmate in the yard. A third convict picked up a bat and hit him over the head. It was a blow that would've killed anybody else. Even the guards were amazed that he could stand. Old Wild Bill just shook his head and shouted, "You son of a bitch." Bleeding like crazy, he raised his fists and got ready to duke it out. But then he came to his senses and relaxed. He was never dangerous.

Alvin Karpavicz, AKA "Creepy" Karpis

I'm frequently asked how Creepy Karpis (AZ-325) came to have his nickname. It was simply that he had an unusual gait: he walked on the balls of his feet, without touching his heels to the floor, so he looked like he was creeping along. Other than that, he wasn't particularly creepy in any way, at least while he was on Alcatraz.

The Birdman of Alcatraz

Robert Stroud (AZ-594) was a killer who constantly tried to manipulate the system and the people around him. A murder he committed in Alaska in 1909 landed him in federal prison, and a second murder, that of a USP Leavenworth correctional officer in 1916, resulted in a death sentence. Thanks to an aggressive letter-writing campaign spearheaded by his mother, President Woodrow Wilson commuted Stroud's sentence to life in prison. After serving thirty-three years, he was transferred to Alcatraz in 1942 and placed directly in one of the D Block isolation cells.

The lethal Stroud engaged in ornithology and bird research while he was incarcerated at USP Leavenworth, but was not allowed this privilege on Alcatraz. The moniker "Birdman of Alcatraz" was bestowed on him by writer Thomas Gaddis, who penned the highly romanticized biography that was later made into a movie.

Stroud claimed that he counseled the warden during the big riot of 1946, a decade before I came to Alcatraz. I highly doubt it. He was living in D Block when the violence erupted, and according to the files, stayed in his cell, barricaded behind mattresses.

Since Stroud was sexually aggressive, we made sure that he never got near other inmates. Initially, he was assigned a cell in D Block, but eventually, he was moved to a cell in the hospital, a rather large cell in fact, with a secure barred door and a secondary wooden door. This kept him from chattering to prison employees during the day. He was allowed out of the cell only when the other convicts were locked up.

Stroud, a vegetarian, was always very concerned about his health. His food regime was peculiar and if allowed, he would cook his own concoctions. For example, it was important to him that vegetables in his stew were fermented, and to make that happen, he added his saliva to the mixture.

On one occasion, he offered some of his vegetable stew to an officer working near his quarters, and the officer agreed to try it. But I had seen Stroud spitting into this mess, and told the officer how he "cooked" the dish. Horrified, he exclaimed, "Holy Christ!" and declined any other offers to share Stroud's vegetable stew.

Stroud sued in federal court for a daily ration of a head of cabbage. The judge allowed him one-half of a head. The Birdman also sued in federal court to have one hour a week alone in the yard. The judge granted the request, but the prison authorities rarely allowed him that freedom.

Stroud exhibited some strange behaviors. For instance, he shaved off every hair on his body, from his head right down to his feet. Since he was not allowed in the showers, he bathed separately in the hospital. He always filled the tub very high, submerged himself, and soaked with just his nose piercing the water's surface.

He was not the inspiring man Burt Lancaster portrayed in the 1962 movie *Birdman of Alcatraz*. Every president and attorney general who came into office—from President Woodrow Wilson to Attorney General Robert Kennedy—looked at his record and decided that Stroud should not be released. Although Gaddis's biography and the movie that was made from it inspired the public to demand that he be set free, prison officials held firm. The decision to put him away forever was non-negotiable and in my mind, it was the right decision. He was a decidedly dangerous man, and I believe he would have continued his murderous and violent ways if given the chance.

Bittersweet Moments

Convicts found companionship where they could. One man, who had charge of garbage collection and disposal, caught a lizard and made it into a pet. He even made tiny costumes for the little reptile, which he kept with him while he worked at the garbage area.

In the course of his duties one day, the lizard happened to fall from his pocket to the ground, and before he could retrieve it, a gull swooped down, nabbed it, and flew off with this man's pet.

From that time on, every time a gull appeared near him, he tried to kill it. He would put bait on a fishhook and swing it out into the air. He hoped a gull, flying in to grab it, would get snagged on the hook. It sometimes worked, and that would be the end of that bird.

Intimate Relationships

Homosexual relationships in the prison did not characterize inmate life in general, possibly because there was so little opportunity for contact. An advantage of each inmate having his own cell was that risks of sexual assault were minimized.

Bill Long remembered an incident in which prisoners coming back from their work in the industries were in transition and entering their cells before the count was taken. Seizing the moment, an inmate—we'll call him Smith—entered the cell of another inmate while the cells were standing open. An officer walked by and saw the two men engaged in a sex act.

When they took him to the prison's court, the associate warden asked Smith what had been going on. Smith explained that he was "just teaching Jessie how to pray." They both went to the hole.

Conjugal visits were unknown at Alcatraz. The only type of visit allowed was one in which each party sat on opposite sides of a small rectangle of bulletproof glass and spoke through a handset.

In order to visit a prisoner, an individual had to contact the mailroom and find out if that prisoner was allowed to see people. Then we checked in with the parole officer for his approval. The FBI helped us verify that the visitor didn't have a criminal record.

Once approved, the visitor entered the front of the prison building and went into a locked area. Facing the inmate, the visitor could see into the cellhouse. Not only did the bulletproof glass keep visitors from passing anything to the convict, but also, officers were not allowed to pass anything to an inmate from a visitor. All contact was very indirect.

Visits didn't happen often. Some of these men had so deeply betrayed their families that relatives wanted no more to do with them. Additionally, many of the inmates were from other states, and the cost of getting to San Francisco, waiting for approval, and finally traveling to the Rock was also a factor.

Face-to-Face but Not Side-by-Side

The racial makeup of the Alcatraz prison population was largely Caucasian and African-American. There were a few Hispanic and even fewer Asian and Native American inmates. In the cell blocks, the races were segregated, with Caucasians in one tier of cells and African-Americans on facing tiers. The system, or some version of it, had been put in place when the prison opened in the 1934, and carried through until it closed in 1963. At the time, it was considered the best way to keep peace among inmates. The men were not segregated anywhere else, however, neither on the job sites nor in the dining hall.

On the Lam

There is sure to be a stir when the public hears of a prison escape attempt, fearing that vicious murderers are on the loose and will threaten them. To us, escape attempts caused distress since it was apparent we had lost control.

USP Alcatraz saw fourteen escape attempts during its twenty-nine-year history. During my tenure (1956 to 1963), I experienced three. Two were truly remarkable escapades, the kind that grabbed the attention of the highest authorities and put dramatic headlines in front of the news-reading public at their breakfast and dinner tables.

Without a wetsuit, swimming in the bay can be an invitation for hypothermia. Even in the summer, water temperatures vary between

50° and 60°F. The tides and currents are also a factor. Prisoners who caught only an hour or two of exercise in the yard daily were hardly in shape swim the distance between the island and the mainland.

When an officer determined that a prisoner or prisoners had tried to get away, he alerted the officer in the control room, who sounded an alarm. This siren, coupled with a steam whistle from the powerhouse, screamed bloody murder; it was powerful enough to awaken and alert everybody on the island that a breakout was in progress. When we heard the escape alarm, we immediately reported to the control center.

Johnson, Burgett, and the Garbage Detail

Clyde Johnson (AZ-864) and Aaron Burgett (AZ-991) had made careers of robberies and escape attempts, but their behavior at Alcatraz had been good enough to warrant assignment to outdoor jobs such as gardening or the garbage detail. Under the supervision of a correctional officer, this team of trusted inmates had a certain amount of liberty beyond the cellhouse to collect and dispose of refuse. Since their responsibilities also included trimming trees and vegetation, they had access to sharpened gardening tools as well.

This particular escapade shows how Alcatraz convicts, even when they were being unlawful, respected their guards. Correctional officer Bill Connor was one of those who had supervisory capacity over the garbage detail. Prisoners valued and liked him.

Garbage detail teammates Johnson and Burgett had been planning their breakout for months, but they had so much regard for Bill Connor that they waited till his work week was over and his relief, Harold Miller, had taken his place. A young man, Miller had been working as a guard for only about ten months, which made him an easy mark by comparison.

On September 29, 1958, while Johnson and Burgett were working outside near the associate warden's house, Johnson pulled a knife on Miller and subdued him. The two then bound his hands, mouth, and eyes with tape and tied him to a tree.

Johnson and Burgett headed for the water. Burgett, robust and much younger than Johnson, waded out ahead, deeper into the water. He planned on swimming and had made paddles out of plywood to help him along. However, he discounted the effect of water on his clothing; as it absorbed water, it began dragging him down.

"I looked at him and he went down like a rock. That was it for me," Johnson recalled. Johnson backed off and sat down on the beach waiting for us to fetch him, which we did.

A couple of weeks later, we pulled Burgett's body out of the water. His face and fingers had been eaten away by sea creatures. The pity was, Burgett was a good man and I had liked him.

When the garbage crew didn't return on schedule, the associate warden knew something was up. He had chosen the inmates whom he considered trustworthy enough to work on the detail and unfortunately, he chose Johnson, who at the time he was arrested was number two on the FBI's "ten most-wanted" list.

The team had been working near the associate warden's house and garden. When the official got to the spot where the two men had last been seen, he looked up toward his house and called out for his wife, but she didn't respond. He was terrified, thinking the convicts had taken her. It turned out that she was visiting a neighbor, but the anxiety he suffered affected his health. He was eventually replaced, and retired not long after.

While you may think these men were evil, they were in fact

prudent. They could have as easily thrown Miller into the water from the heights where they stood, and that would have been the end of him. Instead, they took care to ensure that he was in good condition and, while he was uncomfortable, he wasn't harmed. Even violent inmates usually tried to avoid hurting a correctional officer during my tenure at Alcatraz. Two weeks before that day's escape attempt, Connor and the two inmates had been plying their tasks as usual. In our kitchen, my wife Anna heard people thrashing about, banging garbage cans. She looked out the window and Burgett was working there, looking back at her from just a couple of feet away. When the news about the escape broke, Anna remembered having seen him. "Oh yes, I remember him now," she said. It gave her a chill. Me too.

The Anglin Brothers and Morris

For its sheer audacity, few escapes top the breakout caper of Frank Morris (AZ-1441) and Clarence and John Anglin (AZ-1485 and AZ-1476). It was outrageous enough to inspire a movie, *Escape from Alcatraz*, starring Clint Eastwood.

On June 11, 1962, Bill Long, who was a lieutenant, was supervising six other officers deployed on three tiers to take the routine early-morning count. When the count bell sounded, inmates were required to be standing fully dressed behind their bars, waiting to be checked off.

As was the routine, Bill was waiting on the ground-floor tier, B1, for the officers to come back and report that all was well. But one of the officers was tardy, and Bill was getting uneasy. After an unusual delay of several minutes, Bill saw him approaching from the other end of the hall.

"Bill, I've got a pair I can't get up," he reported. It was rare that two convicts would oversleep, but Bill was not one to shy from a challenge.

Bill said, "I went down to check it. I saw Clarence Anglin lying in his bed and I reached through the bars to touch his pillow. As soon as I touched it, his head flew off! I was shocked. We were all shocked. I backed up and nearly fell, initially thinking that was the man's head. It was obvious that this was a dummy head, but for a second, they caught me by surprise."

Shortly thereafter, they discovered that Clarence's brother John, who lodged in a cell nearby, had left a similar fake cranium behind as a decoy, as had a third inmate, Morris, on the tier above. Three men were missing.

Bill alerted the officer in control, who rang the alarm. "We rushed up to control to get the keys to enter the cells. When we did, we discovered the hole that the two Anglin men had carved for their escape," Bill remembered.

The escapees had penetrated their cells' air vents. Unused for several years, the vents in each cell had been sealed up. They removed the covers and chipped through the sealing material. The openings they carved out over many months led to the roof.

Earlier that night, an officer named Levinson, who was working in the hospital on the top floor, reported that he had been hearing footsteps on the roof above him. Another officer went to check it out, but claimed he had heard no footsteps and could see nothing unusual, Bill recalled.

Levinson said that he had been hearing steps for some time, and he turned out to be right; the convicts had made several trips from their cells to the roof, carrying the equipment they were going to use to get off the island. It took about thirty-five minutes from the time of the alarm to determine what actually happened, Bill said.

It was early morning—around 7 or 7:30 AM—and I was still at home when I heard the escape alarm go off. Along with my other colleagues, I immediately reported to control, where we were told that three men were unaccounted for. Officers were assigned to various points around the island to track them down.

I knew Morris and the Anglin brothers. Morris was extremely intelligent, and many thought he was the brains behind the caper. On the other hand, the Anglins came out of the swamps of Florida. If anybody could survive in the wild, they could.

My duty at that time was to fire up the launch, the *Warden Madigan*. With two other correctional officers aboard, we set out, sailing around the island in expanding circles and keeping a close eye on the water. At the same time, the other launch sailed over to Angel Island to continue the search there.

Within two weeks, we picked up the contents of a wallet, some addresses, notepaper, and pictures. They had kept their keepsakes, their connections to the outside world, in little bags. One of the men's court papers were hovering in the water, just waiting for us to snatch them. In the bay, there's a water separation, a white froth, that bubbles up where fresh water from the Delta and saltwater from the ocean come together. That action kept these items close together and prevented them from floating away. As soon as we salvaged an item, we made an about-face and headed right back to Alcatraz, where we turned over what we'd found to the two FBI agents who were always posted to the penitentiary.

The boat that investigated the water around Angel Island found and brought back a flotation device the convicts had put together, a raft assembled from prisoners' raincoats.

While we kept looking for weeks, we never found the three men, alive or dead. Some still debate whether they successfully escaped or drowned. Given the odds, I think they drowned. At one point, a Norwegian freighter on its way out of the Golden Gate spotted a body and notified the FBI but kept on sailing. It was never totally clear whether or not they picked up the corpse, or who it was.

Parker and Scott

In December of that same year, two other prisoners broke out of Alcatraz. Failing in their attempt, they survived to spend the next several years back in their cells, albeit cells in other prisons.

When Darl Parker (AZ-1412) arrived at Alcatraz in 1959, he was placed in closed-front solitary confinement for having exploded a homemade bomb. He had been frequently disciplined at previous penitentiaries and the pattern continued at Alcatraz.

He had a lot in common with J. Paul Scott (AZ-1403). Violent men, both had robbed banks, stolen merchandise, and made escape attempts during previous incarcerations. They met up again at Alcatraz.

The kitchen storage area, in the basement of the prison, had heavily barred windows, and Parker and Scott took advantage of weaknesses they had discovered in several of the bars. These vulnerabilities had been created by other inmates who, over time, had been trying to cut through the bars.

On the night of December 16, 1962, Scott completed breaking through the bars and returned to signal Parker to follow him through the window on the south side of the kitchen basement. They lowered themselves down to the ground and then reached the water's edge by sliding down a drainpipe. In the drop, Parker broke his foot and sustained deep bruises. They had made flotation devices by inflating rubber gloves pilfered from the hospital, and before getting into the water, they shoved them up their shirt sleeves. Once the two men moved out into the bay, they lost sight of each other.

Incredibly, Scott was carried along by the tide, which was moving at three knots an hour, and washed up onto the rocks under the Golden Gate Bridge near Fort Point. He remarked later that he had been totally unprepared for the severe wave action and the cold water temperatures.

A young soldier and his girlfriend were sitting in a car near the water at Fort Point, where the Presidio meets the south end of the Golden Gate Bridge. As the two looked out at the water, they spotted a body on the rocks. The couple alerted the military police at the Presidio, and when the MPs arrived, they saw that the man was exhausted, bruised, and in shock. Scott was actually near death, with a core temperature 4.6° below normal. He was also almost entirely naked, having been tumbled around to the point of losing his clothes to the wave action. That couple saved his life.

At first, the MPs didn't realize Scott was an escapee, but by the time he arrived at the Presidio's Letterman General Hospital, the word was out, and the doctors realized who they had. Slowly, they brought his body temperature back to normal and within about five hours, he was back on Alcatraz Island.

I was out patrolling in the *Warden Madigan*, looking for Scott, when I got a message from the control center to go to the Fort Mason dock. The army brought him from the hospital to the dock, and loaded him onboard, strapped onto a gurney. When he saw me, he hollered, "Mahoney, why didn't you pick me up faster?"

Parker didn't make it as far as Scott. After he pushed off, he became stranded on what we call "Little Alcatraz," a very small, rocky outcropping near the west side of the island. Our men were shooting at him from the roof of the prison, which kept him pinned down. At the time, I was piloting a regular run of the *Warden Madigan* and had passengers on board. Fortunately, they didn't seem aware of what was going on.

I could see Parker wasn't going anywhere, and using my onboard radio, I told the officers in the towers that they had to quit shooting. But they kept firing, their shots ricocheting off the outcropping's rocky face. I repeated, "You've got to quit it." Finally, they stopped and we were able to rescue Parker. After he was hoisted aboard, we got him to the dock. From there, he went up to the hospital, where they treated his foot.

The prison building dominated the top of the island; in the
foreground are the lighthouse and the warden's house (right).

Guard Bill Long on the gangway to the yard tower.

Guard Jim Langley overlooking the Industries buildings from one of the towers.

ALCATRAZ ISLAND

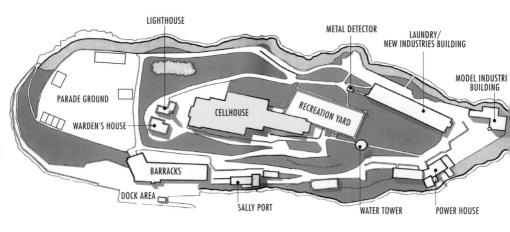

LIGHTHOUSE

METAL DETECTOR

LAUNDRY/
NEW INDUSTRIES BUILDING

MODEL INDUSTRI
BUILDING

PARADE GROUND

CELLHOUSE

RECREATION YARD

WARDEN'S HOUSE

BARRACKS

DOCK AREA

SALLY PORT

WATER TOWER

POWER HOUSE

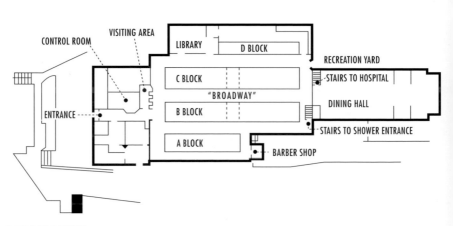

CONTROL ROOM

VISITING AREA

LIBRARY

D BLOCK

RECREATION YARD

C BLOCK

STAIRS TO HOSPITAL

"BROADWAY"

ENTRANCE

DINING HALL

B BLOCK

STAIRS TO SHOWER ENTRANCE

A BLOCK

BARBER SHOP

CELLHOUSE

Looking down "Broadway," between B and C Blocks, toward the entrance to the dining hall.

Guard L. T. "Double Tough" Bordway racking open cell doors.

Sheet laundry and folding operation.

Many inmates passed time in the yard by playing games. The seats were made by the island's Prison Industries workers.

Inmate kitchen worker in the bakery section.

Daily deliveries were handled by trusties (although we didn't trust them much). Everything, including the food, was X-rayed on the dock before being transported up to the prison.

For most of the prison's operation, inmates ate their meals at ten-man tables, which we considered easier to watch than the later four-man tables.

Meals were served cafeteria-style when I was there. Every two weeks, it was "spaghetti day," and one of the inmates always piled his tray high, since seconds weren't allowed.

Crabs picked up near the dock.

AT HOME: FAMILIES AND FRIENDS

Anna and I, Christmas 1962; I'm still wearing my
work uniform.

I f you believe Hollywood and the mass media, you would think that the most common name for the federal prison on Alcatraz was "the Rock." But in fact, the guards, support personnel, and their families who lived on Alcatraz referred to it simply as "the island." Despite its turbulent history and its pull on the public's imagination, to us, Alcatraz was home and our much-loved community.

Family Matters

Although born in the United States, my wife Anna was of Swedish background and served typical Scandinavian food, such as pancakes and meatballs, which our sons and I considered a special treat. We had been married for several years before I realized she spoke and read Swedish fluently. She had never mentioned it and I had never asked. But one day, during an excited conversation with her mother, she responded to her mother in Swedish. I looked at her with surprise and she gave me an embarrassed smile, as though she had been caught in the act.

Anna worked for Fireman's Fund Insurance Company in San Francisco, a job for which she dressed professionally in a dress and high heels. When she came home, she left her work clothes on but put an apron over them; it was important to her to look smart.

The care Anna and I took of our first two-bedroom, one-bath apartment in the ancient Building 64 seemed to be a test of our stewardship. Our neighbors (and prison administrators) could see that I was refinishing the old floors and repainting all the walls, which gave us a good reputation. When newer quarters became available in Building C, we were assigned an apartment on the top floor. The building was located near the edge of the island, and had a great view.

In Building C, we enjoyed three bedrooms and one-and-a-half bathrooms, which came in handy when our family grew to three sons. Steven, who was born in 1957, had his own room, and the twins, born near the end of our time on the island, shared a bedroom. Our rents were far lower than in San Francisco. While people in the city were probably paying $150 or more a month for comparable apartments, we paid $21 a month for our furnished place. But that was a minor benefit compared to what lay outside our windows.

Neither Anna nor I could get enough of the churning life in the water, the sight of the grand city of San Francisco, and the ever-changing cloud formations right outside our door. From our windows, we enjoyed a sweeping view of the Golden Gate Bridge; the hills of San Francisco, Berkeley, and Oakland; and the blue-gray estuary we call San Francisco Bay. We left the drapes open twenty-four hours a day, both for the breathtaking vistas and the fresh sea breeze. There was no worry about privacy; our only neighbors were the wind and the gulls.

Close to the end of our residence on Alcatraz, Anna gave birth to twins, Michael and Patrick. Yes, very Irish names. We weren't expecting two and almost didn't make it to the hospital. Two men helped me get her down the stairs and into the launch; after a successful arrival at Kaiser Hospital, we took delivery of our two surprises.

Mike and Pat were weak at first, and had to stay in the hospital longer than we had anticipated. When we finally brought them home, I changed my schedule on the launch I was working at the time, the Warden Madigan, so I could do the midnight and 3 AM feedings. During the day, she had the help of several of her women friends.

Steve adored his little brothers and was very protective of them.

We put a lot of responsibility on him and he proved good as gold. If we had to leave the house or the car for a few minutes, we would tell him, "Take care of your brothers," and he always did.

Bringing Home the Bacon

While most employees thought Alcatraz was an idyllic community, there were a few inconveniences. One was buying groceries. We had a small store on the island that offered limited supplies of fresh produce, bread, and some meat. But for larger purchases, we had to sail to San Francisco.

When Anna and I first moved to the island, the embarkation point was located at Aquatic Park at the north end of Van Ness Avenue. Two years later, it was moved to the pier at lower Fort Mason, about a half-mile to the west. This was a great boon, because it meant that we could park our cars near the pier. At Aquatic Park, street parking was the only option, and we weren't immune to the occasional break-in.

The new location was also handy in terms of grocery shopping. Lower Fort Mason was less than a block from the city's newest and most modern Safeway. Located on Marina Boulevard skirting the yacht harbor, this was the supermarket the USSR's premier, Nikita Khrushchev, visited on his trip to the United States in September 1959. A couple of months later, Soviet astronaut Yuri Gagarin followed in Khrushchev's footsteps and toured the Safeway as well. I just happened to be out in front of Fort Mason and could see the smallish Gagarin surrounded by security and Soviet diplomats.

Island Infrastructure

The telephone hookups on the island for employees and their family also served the security needs of the prison. While the warden could place telephone calls outside Alcatraz, the rest of us could call only other residents. If any of us had to phone someone off the island, we went to one of four outdoor public pay phones.

However, emergency help would arrive within minutes if someone's handset was knocked off the base of our rotary telephones. When our neighbor Mr. Henry suffered a stroke, Mrs. Henry pulled the phone cord, dislodging the handset; the emergency medical response was almost immediate. This was because a phone left off the hook was intended to be a code in the event that an inmate had taken someone hostage. This never happened, but the code obviously helped.

While we were paid adequately, my colleagues and our families still had to be thrifty, and my ability to fix appliances and make other repairs was appreciated by our neighbors. It also led to more friendships and warmer relationships. I had always been interested in gadgets and novel technology. When we bought the first color television on the island, we attracted a lot more company, which was good, because I needed my friends' help to get it up three flights of stairs; there were no elevators in Building C.

The army's previous occupation of the island meant that we had only direct current (DC), although alternating current (AC) was essential for several kinds of appliances. We all had converters for our AC appliances, and we stowed the motor generator in our closets to muffle the noise.

There was a time when a woman might have been satisfied with a manually operated wringer washing machine, but in the day and age of electric washing machines, there were reasons to be disgruntled. I went to an army-navy surplus store in San Francisco and bought equipment to convert an automatic washing machine to DC from AC frequency, and it was an instant hit. Now we had an electric washing machine, which we kept outside in a broom closet. Word spread, and others often asked to use our washing machine, especially for delicate items. Anna always said yes.

When we had the twins, our laundry burden increased a lot. That's when we started sending our clothes off to the prison laundry, as did all the other employees and their families. The prisoners complained that we sent them more laundry than anybody else. But with three little boys, I was definitely going to take advantage of the service. Laundry would come back not just clean, but folded, too.

Anna made clothes for our boys and I was also able to find an electric sewing machine that could run on AC or DC, so we didn't have to put it on the converter.

A Hearty Social Life

About ninety families and twenty or thirty bachelors lived on the island. Bachelors had quarters in Building A, as did childless couples. Perhaps because we were isolated, we all knew one another, and knew how to have a first-rate good time. We were always looking for an excuse to have a party at someone's home or in the Officers' Club. Of course, by then it was no longer the army's Officers' Club. It was more properly called the social hall, but we often referred to it by the older name.

Anna, who fit into the community like a hand in a glove, helped me host many dinner parties in our apartment. It was a point of pride to present an excellent table for our guests. Men dressed in their good suits and women, in their best clothes. The table settings were formal, with linen tablecloths, napkins, and the good silverware. Even when sharing potluck meals, we always ate at a well-decorated table, set with candles and silver. Occasionally, the warden and his wife would host a get-together for staff and their families, either at their home or the social hall.

I must admit we were part of a clique. Our parties usually included the same fifteen to twenty people. The other people were good folks, but not the same as our close friends. I guess that in the end, we all sort ourselves out according to our own likes and dislikes.

Before I came to work at Alcatraz, convicts worked as waiters in the social hall, but when I was there, we employees waited on tables in the club, something Anna and I did many times.

Occasionally, an employee or employee's wife could not get along with coworkers or neighbors. When such conflict occurred, the family was ordered to live off the island. It was harsh, but it kept the wheels of our institution oiled and turning.

The Officers' Club

The island's social hall was built in 1910 to serve as the army's post exchange. Among its recreational amenities were two pool tables, two bowling lanes, a ping-pong table, and a canteen. It was a valuable place, not only for adults' socializing but also for the children's amusement when they came home from school.

During the nineteen-month occupation of the island by Native American activists in 1970—years after the island was closed as a federal prison—the social hall burned to the ground, as did several other buildings. Many of us regretted the destruction of our former home, particularly for a cause we had difficulty agreeing with.

Holidays, Christmas Trees, and Publicity

Three or four times a year, we had a big island-wide blowout;

Christmas was the occasion for one of them. The lighthouse keeper, the only civilian working on the island, always played Santa. We produced little skits, and some of the children would act in them.

Of course, like any community, we had our share of foolish people. The *San Francisco Examiner*'s yearly Christmas publicity event encouraged readers to notify the paper of some local person's Christmas wish, something that he or she could not fulfill.

The wife of one of the employees on Alcatraz wrote to the *Examiner* that the "poor people of Alcatraz"—and by that, she meant employees, not prisoners—needed special attention during the holidays; she suggested that Christmas trees would be a fine gesture. The *Examiner* granted her wish!

The paper notified the public that they were sending one hundred Christmas trees to the island for its residents, whom the article painted as needy and badly paid, which we were not by a long shot. Warden Madigan was furious. He was very sensitive about the image of Alcatraz and its publicity. But we had to accept the one hundred Douglas fir trees that the *Examiner* and the good people of San Francisco were donating to us. I piloted a special trip to the city to pick up the trees. Very reluctantly, Madigan was on board to accept them officially. I pulled up at the very end of the Fort Mason pier where, with a crane, two or three pallets of trees were lowered onto our bow. As the press filmed, Madigan thanked the *Examiner* briefly but politely. It was very hard on him.

We took the trees back to the island, where the convicts unloaded them. The trees were then stacked outside the social hall for anyone who wanted to take one. Only one person did so, and it was not the person who started the story.

Bill Long exited the social hall at a moment when the trees were being stacked against the outside door. He was disgusted with the rumpus these firs had created, and by the fact that all other employees on the island were reluctant to take one.

"Oh hell, I'm going to take one myself," Bill said, and he carted a tree away. Almost everybody had already bought their Christmas trees, but even if they hadn't, they wouldn't have touched those trees with a ten-foot pole. Coincidentally, Bill had not yet purchased a tree, so he was lucky. After a while, we incinerated the remaining Douglas firs.

Although he was irate, Madigan turned this folly into a teaching moment. He stressed to us once again how important our image was, not just in the Bay Area, but also, worldwide. "Alcatraz is very popular with the press. I've tried to impress this on you people. People listen all the time for stories about Alcatraz," he said.

He frequently cautioned us to say little about our island home or its inhabitants because such tales could be used against us. He often grumbled that when he went to San Francisco, *San Francisco Chronicle* columnist Herb Caen or his assistants would try to contact him or tail him to coax out items for Caen's column, "It's News to Me."

The convicts were usually aware of our holiday parties, and aware that they could not celebrate themselves. But on New Year's Eve, officers would donate their time to go up to the cellhouse and serve the prisoners coffee and doughnuts. On one particular New Year's Eve, I was enjoying some holiday drinking with Bill Long, Bill Connors, and Harold Moore. Then we were notified that nobody was available to serve the convicts their New Year's treat, and urged to come up and do the honors.

I can't say I was eager to pull myself away from our New Year's

Eve party; besides, I was in my suit. But after telling Anna that I'd be gone about an hour, I went up to the cellhouse. The first convict I approached said to me, "Mr. Mahoney, please breathe in my face." I was startled but I did. And since I had been drinking, I must have smelled a little boozy.

"That's the best smell I've ever had," he said. That was repeated about a dozen times with other convicts, with appreciative remarks such as, "That's pretty good stuff you're drinking, Mr. Mahoney."

Meanwhile, other convicts had already finished their doughnuts and coffee and expected me to get around to their cells. I kept trying to leave, but these "deprived" prisoners objected: "No, no, no. He has work to do." They weren't about to be denied of the odor of Jim Beam. I had to oblige them all.

Meanwhile, Anna and Jean Long were in the social hall getting food on the tables and the tables set. By the time I got back, I had probably been gone two hours.

My wife really knew how to organize these parties. Early on, she would be waylaid by people who promised to help out and then never showed up. But she learned to avoid that. When someone volunteered to help out on some future day, she'd write down the statement on two three-by-five cards, one for the volunteer and one for her records. "Here it is. Here's your receipt. This is what you said you'd do for the party that's coming along," she'd tell them. Still, people would occasionally try to backslide, but she'd head them off with the cards: "You have a card. Look at your card." Then she would produce her copy.

Our community also went all out for Halloween parties; even Anna dressed up. Children accompanied by a parent or two went trick-or-treating to every apartment in every housing block, and all the adults had treats ready.

To save money for our big parties, we shopped for supplies at the Goodwill or Salvation Army. I had such an "in" with those people that they'd save practically new candles and other accessories for me. Alcatraz was a golden word that opened many doors. When I entered a store, they'd say, "Here comes Mr. Alcatraz." If the candle cost a dollar or two, I might get it for a quarter. We shopped the same way for children's toys for the Christmas party; some of the products were brand-spanking new.

My Buddy Bill

One of my best friends on the island was fellow officer Bill Long. We first met when I was moving my family's personal effects over to the island on a barge. Employees relocating to the island stacked personal property on a pallet, which was loaded on a barge and delivered to the island's dock. Inmates did the unloading. From there, the new employee had to haul his property to his new apartment.

Bill recalls the event: "I was coming back on the 10 AM boat [from San Francisco] and I saw this guy over there picking up a box. He started toward the stairs and that tipped me off that somebody new was just moving in. So I picked up one of his boxes and followed him in, thinking he might be one of us. Those steps were hard and long. He turned around and saw me, smiled, and asked, 'Who are you?' I helped him bring up the rest of his stuff to the first floor of Building 64, where his apartment was. From that day forward, we were fast friends."

Anna and Bill's wife, Jean, were very compatible, and our families spent a lot of time together. We two couples went out for dinner every second Friday, which was payday. We routinely procured half-price coupons for restaurants and enjoyed the freedom these vouchers gave us to choose among our favorite eating places.

"We played a lot of dominoes to see who was going to buy the first drink when we arrived at the restaurant," Bill recalled. But not just the first drink; we played dominoes to determine which couple would pay for each course, right through the desert and the after-dinner drinks.

Mail Call

By the time we met, Bill's wife, Jean, had become the island's postmistress. The Longs had been friendly with Mrs. Martin, the previous postmistress, and when Mrs. Martin's assistant left the island for good, Jean stepped in on a full-time basis. Six months later, Mrs. Martin died, and Jean moved into her job, serving as the postmistress from about 1954 to 1963, when Alcatraz closed.

In her unique position, she had to sort incoming correspondence for the inmates from that addressed to employees. Bill said that occasionally, a letter landed on Jean's desk that was not addressed to anybody in particular but was written by someone—usually a woman—who wanted to write to a prisoner. However, prisoners could not receive unsolicited mail, only letters from correspondents who had been previously listed and vetted.

A correctional officer was assigned to read and censor all incoming and outgoing mail. One of the things he checked for was references to other prisoners; this was one of our tools for preventing escapes.

One day, Bill recalls, Jean received a little box addressed to the infamous Robert Stroud. It contained a small dead bird. The letter writer explained that she had been raising the bird according to the instructions in Stroud's texts, but the bird had died. Presumably, this lifeless gift was intended to show the writer's scorn for Stroud's scholarship.

But aside from the prisoners, our community was generally a happy family.

Snug at Home

Escape attempts did not threaten our family lives, nor our personal safety. In fact, you could tell from the structure of our living quarters that we were not concerned about security, thanks in large part to the constant presence of about ninety correctional officers (ourselves).

Each of our apartments had a heavy metal door at the front entrance, but our porches, which were attached to the fire escapes leading to the ground, were shielded only by light glass sliding doors. Most residents never locked these glass doors. If a prisoner was going to escape, he'd be very foolish to run toward the homes of the guards. There was just no survival benefit in this.

Nonetheless, household members were given a protocol to follow during escape attempts; as part of that, guards would go to each apartment and take a look around, just to be sure everything was okay.

My son Steven recalled escape alerts during his childhood. "We were told to lock our doors and if anyone knocked, not to open unless you knew exactly who it was. The spouse (fathers and husbands were away looking for the escapees) was asked to look through the peephole and keep everything bolted tightly.

"We were supposed to sit on the couch while officers came into our apartments. Their job was to search through all our closets, underneath the beds, and everywhere to make sure no one was holding us hostage or giving us any problems. I don't remember feeling scared. It was more of a curiosity—it was really interesting that these guys were there, doing what they were doing.

"When those things happened, my dad explained to me that they were worried about an inmate possibly escaping. But we never felt vulnerable. I felt very safe and I never feared the inmates," Steve said.

Building 64, rear view; this is where Steve and his friend
Mike crossed two 2x4s laid across the gap to enter an empty
third-floor apartment.

Bachelor officer quarters on the parade ground.

The canteen stocked most of the basics.

An island luncheon; Jean Long (second from left), Peg Reeves, and Anna (green dress).

Women in funny hats: a joint birthday party thrown for Jean Long (left) and Peg Reeves (right).

Jean, Bill Jr., Pam, and Bill Long.

Jean Long holds our twins, Pat and Mike.

Tom Reeves (front, second from right) at Chillicothe, shortly after Alcatraz closed.

Talent contest at the social hall.

Inmate Blackie Audett serving in the
officers' mess, Christmas 1962.

SECTION THREE

ON THE WATER:
PILOTING THE *WARDEN JOHNSTON*

In front of the *Warden Blackwell*.

In 1956, piloting a 65-foot launch, the transport for the public and inmates, became my passion. In his comprehensive history, Michael Esslinger quotes a story originally printed in the *Foghorn*, the island newsletter: "The *Warden Johnston* was more than a mode of transportation; it was a way of life, our link to the outside world. It took children to school, the sick to the hospital, housewives shopping; it brought food, news, mail, visitors, doctors. In short, it became to the residents as indisputably a part of their lives as their toothbrushes. It was used as a freighter by federal Prison Industries, as a rescue boat for sailors in distress, a gunboat in search of prisoners. It was a link in the transfer and discharge of inmates. It was one of the forces around which local activities revolved."

If there was a serious injury on the island, we made a special trip to bring a doctor over, or to transport an injured person or pregnant wife to San Francisco for care. On the odd occasion when we noticed sailors in distress or even a body in the water, the boat's pilot notified the Coast Guard and then stood by until that force arrived.

There were times when sailboats were in our path. If they failed to detour, we hollered at them with a bullhorn. If the boat approached too close while we were carrying inmates, or came too close to the Rock, one of our crew would take a shot at the front of their craft to alert them that they were in danger. We never hit anything, and didn't try to; the point was to get their attention by sending them the message that we were capable of taking them out. Those steps may seem aggressive today, but at the time, it was the procedure we were required to use. Most of the time, those sailors simply weren't paying attention. But the island was surrounded by buoys; those who sailed inside the perimeter had to know they were in violation.

Powered by a diesel motor, the *Warden Johnston*—named for the penitentiary's first warden—was the workhorse that connected the island with civilian life. We also had an auxiliary vessel that we fired up under extreme circumstances—for instance, in an attempted escape. These launches weighed sixty-five tons, were sixty-five feet long, and could accommodate seventy passengers. We might have pushed that capacity to one hundred during the parties that were held on the *Warden Johnston*.

One day during my early training, while I was working in the kitchen, I was summoned down to the dock where the island's launches were moored. Warden Madigan decided that my mechanical skills would be useful on these boats, since they required constant maintenance.

After I served on two trips, the warden assured me, "You're going to make it." He meant I was going to qualify as a pilot and captain.

I soon realized that I loved this work even more than I enjoyed my other duties on Alcatraz. The job gave me authority and significant responsibility, and I loved feeling that I was shepherding people in safety through dangerous waters. Piloting the *Warden Johnston* became my true calling.

Even more beneficial was the fact that I was doing this job at the same time that I was working on construction for the prison. I started piloting the *Warden Johnston* almost immediately after I got there in 1956. If I were needed on the vessel while I was doing my other job, I would be called away. I earned a lot of overtime; it seemed like I was being paid for two jobs.

I spent as much time with Anna as I could and eventually, with the children, too. Anna could watch me piloting the vessel from our apartment and she would wave me off.

The launch made sixteen turns a day at about thirty-minute intervals, the time it took to get from the island to the Rainbow Pier at San Francisco's Aquatic Park, at the northern end of Van Ness Avenue. It shoved off in the morning at 5:30 AM, or earlier if necessary. Eventually, service was extended to twenty-four hours a day, bringing the number of round trips to twenty.

Earning Coast Guard Certification

At first, I came on board as a relief pilot, working under a Coast Guard-certified captain. While I knew I loved this job, I didn't know if I would be able to advance in it.

One day during this early period, I was talking with Warden Madigan in his office and the teletype machine started cranking out paper. The message was an announcement from Washington, DC.

The warden asked me, "Pat, you know how to answer the teletype message?"

I didn't. He said, "Well, let's go over there and look at it."

Though I was curious, I said, "If it's a message that doesn't pertain to me, I'll walk away."

But it did pertain to me! It said: "P. T. Mahoney Advance Notification." It was the notice of my promotion to motor vessel operator from relief operator. I was thrilled. When my two predecessors left, the prison authorities were in desperate need of someone to take their place. Within a year, I became captain of the boat, which came with a substantial raise. To this day, I don't know if the warden knew what was in the message before it arrived, but I suspect he did.

With that promotion, I had to start a two-and-a-half-month course of study to become certified by the Coast Guard to pilot a vessel that carried a hundred passengers throughout the Bay Area. Madigan allowed me to continue piloting until I passed the test.

Qualifying for a license is a huge challenge, and a tremendous amount of study is required. There was no classroom instruction; it was all done by self-study with materials supplied by the Coast Guard. Thank goodness for my wonderful Anna, who tested me on the material with flashcards. When I was at home, I studied every night; I sometimes even studied while on the boat after we came into port. I'd hit the books for a few minutes while my crew attended to maintenance before we pushed off again.

The course helped me grasp the significance of the buoys with which the bay was dotted. I became familiar with the topography of the sea floor so that I knew when I was steering into shallow waters, and I came to appreciate the expanse of the great estuary we call San Francisco Bay. The estuary is actually made up of three bays—Suisun, San Pablo, and San Francisco—through which flows about 40 percent of California's watershed, from Sacramento and its delta down to San Jose. The material also covered the skills needed to run a boat the size of the *Warden Johnston*, although I had already mastered that during the course of my daily job.

The two-and-a-half day test was administered at San Francisco's Coast Guard headquarters, which was considered to be the toughest exam site. Those who were concerned about passing usually bought a plane ticket to Miami, where the test was said to be much easier.

By the time I finished, I was mentally fatigued. When I finally left the test room, I found Anna waiting and the first thing I said was, "I gotta go to a bar and get a big shot of whiskey to settle me down." I passed on the first try and became a certified pilot and navigator for vessels up to one hundred tons.

Occasionally, I was asked to lend a hand when welding or some other mechanical duty had to be taken care of up high. In those cases, a substitute took my place at the helm.

Maintaining the boats was very labor-intensive; they required a lot of care. On each vessel, we kept three diesel engines shipshape. One powered the fire hoses, the second generated electricity, and the third powered the boat.

Perilous Labor

There was a dark side to this work: we were running unseaworthy vessels, which was illegal. Although my superiors were assured that I was a safe pilot, they could not assure me that our boats were safe to operate. For example, the two vessels were never inspected.

The reason for this negligence was simply that Alcatraz correctional officers had no nautical experience or education. Eventually, the Coast Guard took control of the situation, but at first, I was more or less on my own.

Old-fashioned and below standard, the *Johnston* was powered by a V12. These twelve-cylinder engines, which were originally developed for military aircraft, especially bombers, weighed many tons and were not designed for marine use. Since this engine weighed down the boat's stern two feet lower than it should have been, my predecessors placed concrete blocks in the front of the boat to level it off. This had the net effect of making the *Warden Johnston*'s water line far too high.

What was possibly worse was that we had to sail our launches without radar, depending on compass alone. Piloting the boat in the fog—a weather condition you can count on in San Francisco Bay—was definitely spooky. Every other vessel in the estuary—civilian and military—stopped when visibility was poor. But not us. On the rare occasion, we might see a tug hauling a barge on a very short lead as we sailed on an otherwise deserted bay.

Whenever I approached the island under extreme conditions, I hit the horn. In heavy mist, employees and their families went down to the island's east beach and banged on metal pots and pans to help guide us in. When I heard the clanging, I knew I was getting close.

Even the army and navy, which also had vessels on the bay, told us we shouldn't be sailing. The larger ships (tankers, cargo vessels, and the like) had the apparatus to sail safely in the fog. But we were always in danger of colliding with one of those huge guys.

There were times that we sailed within five to seven feet of a huge transport ship and couldn't see it. I knew it was out there because we could hear it. As I strained to see from the boat's bridge, I kept muttering to my crew (and to myself), "We're getting close. We're getting close." I inched along, navigating very slowly. By the time we were practically alongside it, my crew would caution, "Here it is."

During bad weather, Anna would fret; she would go to the windows and remark, "Oh, there are a lot of whitecaps today."— meaning the sea was rough. My wife watched the *Warden Johnston* disappear in the fog while the north wind was blowing and waited for us to reappear on our return trip. But refusing to sail during bad weather conditions wasn't an option. I would have lost my job, and my family's security was too important to risk it.

The warden, the associate wardens, and the director of mechanical services set the policy and the rules, but they didn't seem to grasp the danger we were in, even though they sometimes rode with us. We spoke to them several times about the perils of navigating the bay without radar, but got nowhere. Their attitude seemed to be, "We've been operating like this for twenty years. What's the big deal?" We were left to operate on dumb luck instead.

The second officer on board handled the ropes to secure the boat so we could power it up to the dock. When the weather was bad and we were wrapped in a blanket of fog, we needed more control and more hands. During those times, I always asked for an additional officer to help us, but the administration didn't always answer the need.

Once, frustrated, I spoke up and said, "When I ask for extra people, it's because I need them. And there's only one person that's going to go to jail if something goes wrong, and that's me, because I'm the one operating under Coast Guard regulations and laws."

Still, nothing came of it. I knew that if my passengers, especially children, were ever injured or lost their lives, I would be charged. Calling the Coast Guard to report on my superiors was out of the question. Not only would I most likely have lost my job, the Coast Guard could have asserted control over when we sailed and when we didn't. That would have been intolerable to the warden.

Overall, I have to say that it was a marvel these vessels were never involved in a tragedy during all their years of service. I was very lucky that my passengers, my crew, and I survived without mishap.

Carrying Prisoners

Prisoners and civilian passengers boarded on the same runs, but were kept separated. We did, however, time prisoner transfers for the middle of the day when children would not be present. Chained to each other at wrist and ankle, inmates were ushered onto the back of the boat; if the weather was bad, they just had to endure it. As the convicts clustered on the fantail outside, passengers could see their legs and feet through the boat's portholes.

In all cases, convicts being transported were accompanied by a deputy with the US Marshals Service, who considered the duty an honor. From the earliest days of the two-centuries-old US Marshals Service (the enforcement arm of the Department of Justice), marshals and deputy marshals were permitted to recruit temporary deputies from the civilian population in order to assist in the transfer of prisoners or the pursuit of fugitives. On a transfer operation, there would be one US marshal, a number of deputy marshals, and some deputized civilians, usually friends or relatives.

I would hop in the marshals' van and accompany them across the bay to Richmond, California, where the train carrying prisoners pulled in. We had the prisoners disembark on the side of the train away from public view, and transferred them into a van labeled US Army.

The deputy marshals were armed, but their deputized civilians were not, and the deputy marshals escorted the inmates on and off the launch. Once all the prisoners disembarked at Alcatraz, the deputy marshals removed their weapons, which were taken up to the tower to keep them out of the prisoners' reach.

Unarmed deputy marshals and their civilian deputies escorted the prisoners closely, while armed penitentiary officers stood at least twenty feet off. The arrangement worked very well until the late 1950s, when a failure to follow procedure ended the practice of having marshals and deputy marshals accompany us.

On that occasion, I jumped in the van in which three deputy marshals and two deputized civilians were waiting, sitting among convicts. Quietly, I asked one of the deputy marshals, "You three are armed, yes?"

He said, "No, we all are."

I was shocked. Weapons, even concealed weapons, were totally against policy for civilians. I responded, "That's why we have people incarcerated in the penitentiaries—they've overpowered and killed people carrying guns."

I accompanied them across the San Francisco-Oakland Bay Bridge and then to the island. After the transfer was complete, I reported the incident to Warden Madigan, who was furious. He immediately contacted the Bureau of Prisons in Washington, DC, and from that moment on, US marshals and their deputies never again set foot on Alcatraz. I felt bad about it because I knew how much these officers and their friends enjoyed the assignment. But we were better off not taking these kinds of chances.

The Boat as School Bus

The *Johnston* was the school bus for children who lived on the island. They were the only youngsters in the Bay Area who had to catch a boat to reach their classrooms. We served about seventy five to eighty grade-school children, thirty high school kids, and several college students each day.

Once the elementary school pupils disembarked, they walked to school with Maryann Wazak, wife of correctional officer Bob Wazak. The Wazaks were among our great island friends. Maryann served as guardian between the boat and the school, and back again in the afternoon. The closest schools for the youngest children were Sherman Elementary School, a public school at Union and Franklin (where our sons went), and St. Bridgid's, a Catholic elementary school at Broadway and Franklin.

The children's safety was always a concern. If the water was choppy, the boat would swing away, which made boarding a challenge, especially for children. In such cases, their little legs might not span the distance between pier and deck, and it was obvious that if a child slipped into the gap and fell into the water, the consequences would be fatal.

Correctional officers worked as crew members, and I always instructed them to take hold of each child's arm as he or she stepped onto the boat. That was the only way we were able to avoid tragedy. But one officer refused to hoist the children as I instructed. Retired from the military, he'd served his country but rejected my instruction. I laid down the law: "You must grab their arms." But he would just stand there, frozen. When I insisted, he responded, "I don't care."

I said to him, "Then you don't work here anymore," and immediately called the warden's office and had him transferred to another post. He was shocked, and his reply revealed his basic misconception: "I don't work for *you*." Wrong.

"You said it right there, you don't work for me," I affirmed.

The person who replaced him surely must have thought, "Thank goodness that guy goofed up, because I've got his job now." Working on the boats was a plum job for Alcatraz personnel, and this unwise officer regretted his decision; he later asked for his job back. But I'm glad I didn't relent.

Finally, after we got a whole new breed of vessels, I devised a gangplank that moved on rubber tires and locked onto the boat. From then on, we didn't have to fret quite so much as these little people boarded and disembarked. It was also nice to receive a $500 award from the warden for this innovation. I was mighty proud and so was my family.

Sad Duties

The *Warden Johnston* and its successors occasionally served as hearses as well. When someone died on the island, the only way to get the body to San Francisco was by transporting it on the launch.

Bill Long remembered a time when we narrowly avoided an unpleasant accident. One of our colleagues passed away on the island, and Bill and three other officers carried his body in a steel basket to load it onto the boat for transport to the city. I was busy maneuvering the boat up to the dock.

As Bill recalled, "We set [the basket] on the rail momentarily, preparing to set it down [on the boat]. The boat suddenly lurched as a wave came by. Fortunately, we were alert, and grabbed and saved the body just in time. Otherwise, we would have lost him in the water."

New Boats at Last

Eventually, the Coast Guard and the military were able to put enough pressure on the BOP to modernize our fleet, and we were able to upgrade our boats.

Someone at Alcatraz got in contact with the navy and the army and learned that new P-51s were available. The armed forces had an overstock of ten to twenty of these vessels, which had been designed for cargo and constructed for the Korean War. We acquired two and converted them to passenger use. These were modern vessels, up to standard and, best of all, equipped with radar.

Then came the circus of naming them. By this time, Madigan had retired and Warden Olin G. Blackwell had taken his place. Blackwell insisted that one of the vessels be named after him. But to put a good face on this display of vanity, he named the other one *Warden Madigan*, after his much-honored predecessor.

The dock was an active area, and the guard on duty in the dock tower was kept busy monitoring its activities; he also controlled the key to the launch.

Pulling into the dock at lower Fort Mason.

Inmates on the Alcatraz dock ham it up for the camera.

The *Warden Johnston* (I'm in the pilot house).

School kids lined up for a ride to San Francisco.

Guard Wardren and his wife at the Fort Mason dock, where prison employees who lived on the island stored their cars.

The *Warden Blackwell* at the Fort Mason dock; I received a $100 award for designing and building the gangway.

THE LAST BOAT OUT

Looking back at Alcatraz from the prison launch, circa 1963.

One day in 1963, I was at the helm of the *Warden Madigan*, carrying two Bureau of Prisons officials to the penitentiary. As usual, they rode with me on the bridge, and we talked. That's how I became the first correctional officer to know that Alcatraz was closing down. This news was a blow to me. I had truly thrived during my years at Alcatraz—it was the high point of my career—and it was also the place where Anna, the boys, and I became a family.

Soon after, BOP Deputy Director Merle Alexander visited from Washington, DC, and told everyone that Alcatraz would be shutting down. I said to Merle, "Everyone needs an Eiffel Tower to brag about. Alcatraz is the Bureau of Prisons' Eiffel Tower." Years later, Merle told me he'd remembered my words.

Some of my colleagues wanted to leave the island anyway; many hoped to go back to their home states and work for the BOP there. But I took it really hard, as did Anna and Steve. There were a lot of tears. It had been an exciting place to work and live, and we felt rooted in our community.

At first, we thought the Morris-Anglin escape might have been the deciding factor, but it turned out that the BOP had been planning this move for months before that breakout. Several things influenced the decision: Alcatraz was expensive to run; per day, it cost about three times as much to support a prisoner on the island as compared to other prisons in the country. The fifty-year-old cement prison building, which was older than its years thanks to the marine climate, was becoming dilapidated and difficult to maintain, and would have been expensive to restore. Furthermore, it was hard for the BOP to manage public relations. For instance an outsider, like a reporter, had to have special permission to talk to the warden, but only the DOJ could furnish the control number that gave an outsider access to a penitentiary official. Plus, people who lived in Bay Area had never been particularly happy about having a maximum-security prison nearby, and every crisis on the island reaffirmed their fears.

It was indeed a fact that Alcatraz attracted intense press interest, and some of our top officials couldn't stand the pressure. It certainly upset Warden Blackwell, who was nervous about talking to the press. If a mishap occurred at any other penitentiary, it remained local news. But if it happened at Alcatraz, the world knew about it.

Once, after an escape attempt, I happened to be working in the control center when Drew Pearson called in to speak to the warden. A '40s and '50s-era muckraking journalist and broadcaster, Pearson built his reputation on his exposés of public figures, especially politicians. He said he had gotten a control number directly from the DOJ; in other words, he went over the head of the Bureau of Prisons entirely. This was unprecedented in my experience.

I called the warden and said, "This is Drew Pearson himself— not his secretary—on the line. He says he has a control number from Justice and wants to talk to the warden." This was just too much stress for Blackwell.

Finally, US Attorney General Robert Kennedy decided to shut our prison down. The public found out about the closure almost the same time that staff did. All the newspapers ran the story: "ALCATRAZ TO CLOSE."

The convicts learned very quickly that their prison had a limited future. Most of them were relieved that they were going to "get out of this damn place." They knew they'd be going to another facility where they would have more freedom and privileges, a difference of night and day for them. But there were a few who weren't happy—

they'd miss the exceptional food.

Deputy Director Alexander brought with him an official from the BOP's human resources department, who instructed the personnel staff to consult with employees on their next career steps. It was about three months between the time of the announcement and our actual departure. I knew that I was assigned to go to the new penitentiary at Marion, Illinois, and I wasn't happy about it.

Over a period of several weeks, groups of convicts were transported to San Francisco International Airport, where buses carried them out to the tarmac. This was done to keep them away from the airport interior and public view. On one occasion, a plane carrying inmates had to make a temporary landing in Albuquerque, New Mexico. When the city's aviation authorities became aware of its presence on their turf, they contacted local law enforcement and dozens of policemen roared to the airfield. I don't know what they thought our convicts were going to do—chained together, they were unlikely to storm the airport.

Predictably, news of Alcatraz's closure went worldwide. Newspaper and network reporters came from around the globe to document the final parade of prisoners from the prison to the launch, and only the most senior correspondents were assigned to cover it. Drew Pearson was certainly there, as was Herb Caen. By the time they came to cover the last boat taking prisoners out—which I piloted—there were only twenty-seven convicts left. But the photos of these men exiting the penitentiary and filing onto the gangplank were plastered on front pages everywhere.

On the trip that took the last of the convicts from Alcatraz to the mainland, I didn't have time to worry about the press or what the convicts were saying to them as I navigated the boat against a strong north wind. I also didn't have the luxury of saying "See you later" to this one or that one. Press people were everywhere—both on the boat and on the San Francisco dock—and they were all clamoring for quotes and interviews.

For "treasure hunters" reading this book: Among the items we later ferried from the island to the mainland were two small, heavy, wooden ammo boxes full of keys—keys to the cells, the offices, virtually all of the locked areas of the prison—which we were instructed to dump in the bay. I didn't want to do it, but about halfway between the island and the mainland, I followed orders and over they went. The guards kept a few as souvenirs, but most are still out there. (Other things had been going into the bay for a long time—for example, the cells had saltwater toilets, and the cellhouse sewer line emptied directly into the bay.)

In Michael Esslinger's book, there's a quote from inmate Frank C. Weatherman (AZ-1576), who was asked by a reporter how he felt about the prison closing. Weatherman, the last convict to come onto USP Alcatraz Island and the last one off it, is reported to have said, "Alcatraz was never no good for anybody." That sure wasn't how I felt.

When all the prisoners had finally left, staff entered the cellhouse to make sure no one remained. As we started unloading ammunition and arms, I looked up at the officer in the tower and saw him looking down at me as he carefully lowered rifles, carbines, pistols, and a projectile called a Gaskin in a canvas carrier so they wouldn't be damaged. Then I watched him come down the spiral stairway and lock the tower gate. But nothing else was secured, because nothing meaningful was left.

Guard Jim Albright (light suit) escorts inmates off the
launch on March 21, 1963, the prison's last day.

AFTER ALCATRAZ

The island at dusk.

During the three-month period leading up to evacuation, I packed up tools and equipment and sent them off to the facility in Marion. Since I ran the machine and welding shops, I oversaw the bundling of large machinery, which was sealed in oversize boxes and strapped with heavy metal bands. We stamped USPAZ on every box.

One day during this shutting-down period, I was working on the *Warden Madigan*, up on the bridge behind the pilothouse. The electric circuit breaker had kicked out, and we lost lighting. Tearing back to reset it, I hit a wet patch on the floor and fell headlong over the ladder and down the stairs into the engine room. Although I sustained a painful injury to my back, my doctor told me I could proceed with my plans to vacate prisoners and family from the island.

Once the prisoners were gone, I hired some young men to pack up my family's household goods, supervising them from in a chair in our apartment. It wasn't long before our furniture and the rest of our belongings were on their way to Marion, Illinois.

Meanwhile, my colleagues and their families were so busy packing and getting ready to go that there was no time for celebrations or sendoffs. We didn't all leave the island at once, however; though some left right away, my family and I took off about a month after the prison closed.

When the lights finally went off on Alcatraz, it was a very somber feeling. At the time, we were across the bay from the island, and I could barely stand to look back at the place. It was painful.

Our car was parked at lower Fort Mason as always, and I loaded up the few things we were carrying, and made sure the children were settled. Then the five of us made our way to nearby Vallejo, where we stayed overnight with my brother. The next day, we shoved off and made it to Reno, Nevada.

It was not a great trip. A drive that should have taken two days took five because I was in such pain from the fall on the boat. Finally, we stopped in Grand Junction, Colorado, where I ended up having surgery. After a four-month convalescence, I was able to travel, and we went on to Marion. (That fall left me with a major physical issue for many years.)

Once I got to USP Marion, I was taken aback to find that the machinery and equipment I had sent ahead was missing. In my absence, the packages that I had carefully labeled USPAZ had been emptied. Sitting there at Marion, unattended, they had proven to be an attractive nuisance. Deeply intrigued, everyone—from inmates to staff—wanted to see what was in those big cartons; even the correctional officers and the lieutenant were curious. Finally the pressure became too great and the containers were opened. And that was the end of that: everyone wanted souvenirs from the notorious federal penitentiary at Alcatraz, and the contents—down to the screwdrivers—were removed. When I finally came on the scene and found that all of my tools and equipment had disappeared, I was furious.

The chief of mechanical service apologized to me. "Pat, I tried. But they were so intrigued by those boxes I knew sooner or later they were going to get into them."

We made up a list, and I then ordered brand-new tools. I had the vendors mark the box: "In care of the Warden, US Penitentiary, Marion, Illinois. Attention Mechanical Services: Pat Mahoney." That did it.

After years of service at Marion, I was transferred to the US penitentiary at Lompoc, California, in 1967, and retired in 1979. In the years since, my precious Anna has died and my friend Bill Long recently joined her. I take comfort in my wonderful memories of those seven years during which we held together as family, friends, and community.

And for what purpose? I sincerely feel that we were protecting not only the American public, but also our desperate convicts from themselves. My experiences dealing with the prison system and convicts gave me an instinct for order and service that I like to think I passed on to my three fine sons.

But of all the things I miss about Alcatraz, probably what I miss the most is coming home at the end of my shift, bursting with stories and being able to say to Anna, "You won't believe what happened today."

REMEMBERING ALCATRAZ: CHILDHOODS ON THE ROCK

Anna made Steve and I matching jackets;
1960.

I wasn't the only one in my family to experience life on Alcatraz. The children of employees enjoyed their own special world on the island. —P.M.

The Guard's Son

By Steven Mahoney, Colonel, US Army (ret.)

Born on Alcatraz in 1957, I lived there my first six years until the prison closed in 1963. My memories are those of a little boy who created his own fantasies of danger while safely protected from the most depraved convicts in the country. I've traveled back to the island many times to keep these memories alive.

The grounds, the property, and buildings on the island loomed far larger in 1960 than they do today. They were thrilling, mysterious, and demanded investigation. With my friends Mike Wazak and Kenny Albright, I played games inspired by the notoriety of the desperate men who lived on our island. The parade ground, Building 64, the eucalyptus grove near the water, and the shoreline itself were our domains, our kingdoms to explore and rule. Of course, our parents put limits on our explorations, but they couldn't entirely dampen our drive for discovery.

The Eucalyptus Grove

On its eastern end, the island drops off vertically to the shoreline, and at the time, a tall fence separated a thicket of eucalyptus trees and cacti from the dock. We were not allowed to play there, but we sneaked in, making our way between or around the apartments that stood above the slope, through the trees, and down to the shore. I doubt we were as tricky as we thought: the sap from the eucalyptus trees had a strong menthol odor and we reeked when we came home.

When it came to stealing into and out of this mysterious area, timing was everything. We needed to hide from the guard tower looming above, and if boats were coming in or out, or anyone was working on the dock, we also risked exposure.

We usually brought pieces of bread to toss to the fish and crabs, and occasionally, we saw a three- or four-foot shark. The sharks never seemed particularly interested in our groceries, however.

Our parents fretted because the shoreline was risky. Tides came in and out with unexpected speed, and they could carry away a little person if one of us got too close. Fortunately, nothing happened to us, and a handful of flowers from one of the overgrown gardens was sufficient to keep my mom from fuming over my adventures.

During very low tide, we'd follow the shoreline around the curve of the island. Eventually, we reached a little beach, a flat area with small stones and sand. At this point, we made sure to keep an eye on the tide to avoid getting stuck there. In reality, we could never have circled the entire island, but we thought of it as a worthy goal.

A View from the Dock

It was exciting to be on the *Warden Johnston* and on the dock. Today, when I return to Alcatraz, I can spot the slips where boats docked when the island was an active prison. Usually, my dad was captain when I rode the ferry, but I knew better than to divert his attention from his job. But occasionally, he gave me a tour of the boat and took me down to the engine room.

For an adult, getting off the boat was an easy process, but the gap between the deck and the dock loomed large to me as a small child. I was always concerned about slipping into the water and becoming a shark's breakfast. It would've been more likely that I would've drowned or been injured by the boat or the rocks, but my mind was clearly focused on the risk of being gobbled by a shark. Usually an adult would hold my hand to cross the gap.

A Special Visitor

Every school day, I took the *Warden Johnston* to San Francisco and back. A woman visitor often made the same trip, and I saw her onboard. Even at six, I knew she was beautiful, and her glamour, blonde hair, and fur coat distinguished her from the other passengers.

At some point, we started talking, and during one of these chats, she told me that she would bring me some candy. And on the next trip, she did! I was thrilled that she remembered her promise to me. Years later, I found out that she was the girlfriend of the notorious gangster Mickey Cohen. According to the *Los Angeles Times*, her name was Sandra Hagen (originally, Clarita Has Hagen). I just knew her as a nice adult who had given me candy, something we could never have too much of as kids.

Mountain Climbing

If you stand on the dock and look at the island's various landmarks, you'll notice a cliff immediately in front of you. When I was a child, it seemed to be thousands of feet high. A curious set of stairs, actually a bulwark, rises up that cliff. Its shallow steps made it hard to ascend, but I couldn't resist. Occasionally, I would ask my dad if I could climb the stairs, and he usually said no. Once, however, he gave me permission, apparently believing that I could not make my way very far up. Then he turned his attention to another adult, falling into conversation.

I scampered up to the top. I didn't dare look down, but—proud of what I had done—I shouted to my dad, who must've been shocked to see where I was. I was surprised to see that he was quite angry. When I climbed down, he made sure I understood I was never to climb up that bulwark without him watching. He said I needed to yell to him when I reached the halfway mark if he was not looking.

When I saw Steve up on that ladder at the top of the hill, I was furious—he could have been killed. But he was always adventurous. One time, he and a friend climbed up the fire escape to another couple's apartment because he heard they kept chocolate milk. (We didn't carry chocolate milk in our house.) Steve and his friend entered their apartment, went to the refrigerator, and helped themselves. When I found out, I told him not to do it again—that it was "non-negotiable." That was a word Steve and his brothers came to understand. —P.M.

The Parade Ground

The army had created a parade ground at the west end of the island, but during the BOP era, it was rarely used for anything official. This paved expanse became our play area, an open space on which we could ride our bikes, fly kites, play softball, and do anything else our imaginations allowed.

Flying our homemade kites was difficult at first. The gales on the island are strong, and we didn't know how to balance kites for big gusts. Some days, the winds were more forgiving, and that's when we competed to see who could get his kite the highest. It wasn't uncommon for our light strings to break, leaving us watching helplessly as our creations made their way into the bay. Eventually, we learned from older kids to attach small weights onto the kites' tails so that a gust would pull the kite up and carry it farther away from the island before it hit the water.

In another attempt to take advantage of wind power, we collected large pieces of cardboard and old sheets. We made the cardboard into little flat carts and then sat in them, holding on to the four corners of the sheet until a draft of wind blew us across the field. It wasn't very fast, but it was fun. Eventually, we transferred this sheet technology to our wagons, which made for a lot faster ride.

When I raced across the parade ground on my first bike (complete with training wheels), I felt an enormous sense of freedom. Later, I was terribly proud when the training wheels came off and I could go even faster. My buddies and I flew back and forth across that cement pad.

We played lots of hide and seek and sometimes pretended that we were soldiers. We were not allowed to have toys that looked like handguns, but I did have a toy rifle that fired caps and a toy cannon that fired plastic cannonballs. This pretend warfare made me feel as though I was a hero, inspired by television programs such as *The Rifleman* and other Westerns of the day.

Nearby, in a large sandlot, there was a teeter-totter, jungle gym, and swings. Next to the sandlot was a handball court with a small weight-lifting area. We were not supposed to go in there, but had no problem slipping in and having fun when the door was left unlocked. We'd climb on a chair to hit the boxing bags, feeling ourselves to be quite big and tough after our effort.

My most poignant memory of the parade ground had nothing to with my pals. One of my chores was to go to the commissary when my mom needed groceries. Although I was a little kid, it wasn't a difficult task. One day, I was bringing home milk and some canned goods. The bag was heavier than normal and the wind was stronger than normal and I was having a hard time making headway. About halfway across, the bag fell apart and all the cans spilled out. I just gave up, sat down, and began to cry from frustration. My mother saw me from our apartment. Grabbing a basket, she put on her raincoat, came down, picked up the scattered groceries, and escorted me home. Back in our apartment, she made us hot chocolate to warm up. It was the best hot chocolate I have ever had.

Meeting the Neighbors: Convicts

We were not to approach or speak to prisoners in any way. But this didn't keep us from exchanging a simple hello. Once, I passed a candy bar through a fence to a convict on a work crew. He seemed appreciative, and we talked for a few minutes about the pleasant weather. He asked me how I liked school, and told me to study hard or I'd end up in prison like him. He then turned back to his work. I never found out who he was, but his words stayed with me.

Occasionally, we saw prisoners on their work details gardening or cleaning up certain areas. Sometimes they were stationed near the bachelor quarters on the other side of the large fence near which we were playing. We weren't supposed to, but we played near that fence within earshot of the prisoners and frequently talked to the convicts. They addressed us as any adult would a child. "Hello, how are you?" To be answered by: "I'm fine, how are you?" Once, an inmate asked me if I had a cigarette or if I could get him one. I was four or five at the time so his request just seemed strange to me.

Special Places

There was no question: children never entered the prison. We tried to approach the front entrance, although we weren't allowed beyond a certain point. In fact, there were several places on the island we were not allowed to enter: near the utility work area and the old and new Industry buildings, primarily. A nearby guard tower made it hard for us slip into these taboo places. Most of the time, these prohibited areas were closed off, but every now and then, someone would leave a gate or some other access open.

This was our chance to explore the mother lode of scrap materials, the old Model Industries building outside the perimeter of the main prison. Here, we found wood, nails, screws, rope, and other scrap that we used to build things. Getting in required us to crawl along the path, waiting for the guard to turn his back. Then we ran like the dickens to get past his view. He sometimes saw us and yelled at us to get back. But we were successful often enough to make it worth our while to test the system.

Home Sweet Home

Building 64, originally built as an army barracks during the late nineteenth century, was designed in the most haphazard way. Some said there was paranormal activity there, but I surely never saw a ghost.

When we walked up the stairs to our apartment, we had to pass through a gate opened by a guard in the tower. Our unit was a couple of doors down from the commissary and post office. We lived there when I was very small, and I remember Christmas in that apartment, and a big tree. The bathtub seemed huge.

With my friends, I sometimes played on the walkway in front of the apartments, several stories above the ground. We'd drop pebbles of various sizes and watch to see if the larger pebble took longer than a smaller one to land. We thought that larger pebbles would fall faster; we didn't know the word "physics" at the time, much less were we familiar with its concepts. Definitely bunch of budding Isaac Newtons.

One day, while exploring the upper level of Building 64, Mike Wazak and I noticed a vacant apartment and decided to look around. We came upon a couple of boards, which we nailed together. This worked perfectly as a ramp and allowed us to walk across the gap from the top walkway into a window. I'm amazed now that neither of us was hurt. I recently went back to the same location and found that the gap was more than ten feet wide. We were young and thought we were invulnerable, but were actually just plain lucky to not be hurt that day. At any rate, we opened the window, went through it, and entered the apartment. All the rooms were empty; we played for hours with our toy soldiers in our secret encampment. This lasted a few weeks until we noticed packing boxes appearing and realized that someone was about to move in. That ended a chapter of escapades.

If you stand on the uppermost walkway behind Building 64, you can look down on a two-story corridor we called "Chinatown." When families were doing laundry or when the fog was in, this metal-plated passageway steamed up and appeared to be an entirely different and mysterious world. When it was dry, we played above it, tying strings to the grates that lined the walls on its upper floor. The strings hung down to the ground below. Our G.I. Joes and other toys had many a ride on these strings.

New Digs

Later, we moved to a larger apartment on the top floor in Block C, a newer apartment building for the guards and their families. We had a view of the parade ground from our dining room window, and of downtown San Francisco from our living room. Even as a small child, I thought that was remarkable. I have to say, however, after a while I took this magnificent view for granted.

Our front door was very strong and meant to keep anyone from breaking in. A small peephole looked into the hallway. I remember discussing with pals Mike Wazak and Kenny Albright how silly it seemed to have such a strong door at the entrance when anyone who wanted to break in could easily climb the fire escape to our patio area and come through the sliding glass doors.

On the Fourth of July, we watched the fireworks from our apartment. The San Francisco skyline lit by the display was an even more amazing sight, and the view was better than from the city itself. When the weather was warm, we picnicked on the parade ground.

I liked having my friends over to our place, and my parents were always very welcoming to them. My family had the first color television on Alcatraz, which made me quite popular. I remember my dad and his pals carting it up our waxed steps. (My favorite show was *Howdy Doody*.) Among the stories from my childhood that my mother liked to tell was the time we were planning my birthday party and I made sure she knew that I wanted her to invite "lots of pretty girls." I was only five at the time, so it made a good story for my parents to share with others.

We enjoyed many parties at the social hall. I especially remember the Halloween that I dressed up as a tiny cowboy. My mom was not pleased when I showed up at my parents' table soaking wet from bobbing for apples. I was very pleased with myself until I saw how unhappy she was with my wet clothes.

School

When I entered school, I was taken to the principal's office and introduced as a child from Alcatraz; we also had to have dog tags to identify ourselves. The prison authorities took these simple precautions to safeguard against a potential kidnap or hostage situation. (Also, there was a concern that if we became lost, people wouldn't believe us if we said we lived on the island; I still have that tag, which is embossed with my name and address.) That never happened, but I enjoyed the little extra attention we got because of where our fathers worked.

The MTA's Son

By Tom Reeves

"Mr. Mahoney." That's how we addressed Pat Mahoney when we were teenagers.

When my dad, Thomas Reeves, and stepmother brought me from Idaho in 1959, Mr. Mahoney was the first Alcatraz officer I met, and I met him on the boat. I had come to San Francisco to visit my father; my stepmother, Peg; and my brothers, Jack and Earl, during the Thanksgiving holiday, preparatory to moving to the island during the Christmas holiday.

Living on Alcatraz, you quickly realized that your only links to San Francisco and the rest of the world were the Alcatraz launches *Blackwell* and *Madigan*. Without "Mr. Mahoney," we were stuck.

I was a kid from Idaho with limited exposure to the world. After my parents divorced, I spent most of my time working on my stepfather's farm. By the time I was nine, I had a social security number; by ten, had moved miles of irrigation pipe, and by eleven, was operating a tractor and trucks. Coming to Alcatraz, however, was totally out of my realm of comprehension. Knowing people like "Mr. Mahoney" made the transition bearable.

The island was like a small town, and there was quite a camaraderie among those who lived there. On occasions when we all got together, my brother Jack and I were asked to look after the little guy (Steve) to make sure he did not get hurt. Frankly, on the island, there were very few places to get hurt, unless you got stuck down in China Alley or on the beach among the century plants.

My brothers set pins in the Brunswick two-lane bowling alley at the social hall. My older brother, Earl, and his friend Phil Dollison reported that they got ten cents a game from the Officer's League, which bowled once a week. After my brother and Dollison moved off the island, the guys in my age group, including my brother Jack, were paid twenty-five cents a game.

We spent a lot of time at the social hall, and during my time on the island, I became a fairly good pool hustler (I took this skill to the mainland, where I was able to use it to make a few bucks). I'm sure many young Alcatraz residents, male and female alike, surprised their friends with their pool and billiard skills. We had time to develop them since there wasn't much else for teenagers to do. On Sundays, we occasionally went to the hall to watch the movie the inmates had seen the previous night, and three or four times a year, there would also be social events, potluck dinners and sometimes live entertainment. The wives usually got most of organizational duty.

There were not a lot of teenagers on the island while I was there, maybe fifteen between the ages of fourteen and eighteen. Some of those teenagers were friends. I know that my younger brother, Jack, was close to several of the guys. It used to be great fun for Jack, and occasionally me, to head into Chinatown with a gang of Alcatraz kids, hopping aboard the 30 Stockton bus or the Powell/Hyde cable car near Fisherman's Wharf. Most of my friends were kids whose parents were stationed at Fort Mason or who lived in the Marina District.

The Marina was the basic stomping ground for the Alcatraz kids, and we knew almost every shop on Chestnut Street. Model shops provided hours of entertainment when we finished our homework, and we got our after-school sugar fix at Hunt's Donuts. On Friday or Saturday nights, we could be found at the movie theater or one of the several Italian restaurants. (The last place I wanted to be on Friday or Saturday night was Alcatraz.)

North Beach was another of our stomping grounds, and my preferred venue back then was City Lights Bookstore. Lawrence Ferlinghetti, the poet and City Lights founder, published Beat generation authors, and I loved to watch the happenings at the bookstore; I discovered poetry through Ferlinghetti's *Coney Island of the Mind*. For a kid from Idaho, these experiences were life-changing.

When I was in ninth grade at Marina Junior High School, I came up with a little enterprise to make money. I wasn't afraid to work, but as a teenager living on Alcatraz, there was no work I was permitted to do, except for setting pins. So I invented my own job. At school, I signed people up to come to the island on Saturdays, and sometimes Sundays as well. The trip cost a dollar. I'd pick up my "guest" at Fort Mason's Pier No. 2 waiting room, and send him or her back on the next boat, an hour later. On a typical Saturday, I had as many as ten "guests." If curiosity at school was high, I could make as much as twelve to fourteen dollars on a weekend.

On the sign-up sheet, kids would tell me the times they would like to come over to the island. I would leave their names and the time of their visit with the guard at the entry to lower Fort Mason at Bay Street and the Marina Boulevard gate. Most of the kids came through the Safeway store at Marina Boulevard. The key point was, they came. This was my business and I didn't care which gate.

After about seven months of this tour guide business, someone "outed" me to the warden. As I sat on the edge of the bathtub in our apartment bathroom, my father firmly explained to me that my behavior—running a business on the island—was wrong and subject to a punishment, a punishment that could force families off the island. Since my dad was required to stay on Alcatraz, this could mean our family would have to split up, with him living on the island in the bachelor's quarters and the rest of us living in the city. This was obviously not acceptable. I agreed to stop my tour business. I was then required to write a brief note apologizing to the warden for my infraction.

I always laid the blame for my business interruption on Mr. Mahoney, because he was the one who was usually running the boats. However, recently, while sharing a few shots of Jameson's with him and his family, he assured me that it wasn't him—it had to have been the Wildcat, he said. I believed him, mainly because I think he had enough to drink that night that he wouldn't have been able to keep his story straight unless it were true.

Pat is getting older, but to me, he is still "Mr. Mahoney."

The parade-ground duplex was occupied by the associate warden and the captain of the guards.

A young Steve Mahoney (front left) and pals.

Taking in a children's program; Steve Mahoney (second row,
with bow tie), Bill Long, Jr. (fourth row, right).

Reeves family, 1962.

Alcatraz kids at the playground; Steve is at left.

More Alcatraz kids; Bill Long, Jr., is at left.

Suggested Reading

Albright, Jim. *Last Guard Out: A Riveting Account by the Last Guard to Leave Alcatraz*. Bloomington, IN: AuthorHouse, 2008.

Babyak, Jolene. *Breaking the Rock: The Great Escape from Alcatraz*. Oakland, CA: Ariel Vamp Press, 2001.

———. *Eyewitness on Alcatraz: Life on the Rock as Told by the Guards, Families, and Prisoners*. Oakland, CA: Ariel Vamp Press, 1988.

Esslinger, Michael. *Alcatraz: A Definitive History of the Penitentiary Years*. Marina, CA: Ocean View Publishing Company, 2003.

———. *Letters from Alcatraz*. Marina, CA: Ocean View Publishing Company, 2008.

Gregory, George. *Alcatraz Screw: My Years as a Guard in America's Most Notorious Prison*. Columbia: University of Missouri Press, 2008.

Heaney, Frank. *Inside the Walls of Alcatraz*. Self-published, 1987.

Lageson, Ernest. *Guarding the Rock: A Father and Son Remember Alcatraz*. San Francisco: Golden Gate National Parks Conservancy, 2008.

Martini, John. *Alcatraz at War*. San Francisco: Golden Gate National Parks Conservancy, 2002.

Odier, Pierre. *The Rock: A History of Alcatraz: The Fort/The Prison*. Eagle Rock, CA: L'image Odier, 1983.

Quillen, Jim. *Alcatraz from Inside: The Hard Years 1942–1952*. San Francisco: Golden Gate National Parks Conservancy, 1991.

Stuller, Jay. *Alcatraz: The Prison*. San Francisco: Golden Gate National Parks Conservancy, 1999.

Ward, David, and Gene Kassenbaum. *Alcatraz: The Gangster Years*. Berkeley: University of California Press, 2010.

Wiener, Leigh. *Alcatraz: The Last Day*. San Francisco: Golden Gate National Parks Conservancy, 2012.